MAKING THE DIFFICULT AND CHALLENGING JOURNEY TO "MAINSTREAM AMERICA"

A Journey Worthy of Consideration

Harvey J. Coleman

Book Savvy International Inc.
Success is waiting for you...

Copyright © 2024 by Harvey Coleman

All rights reserved.

No part of this publication may be reproduced in any form, by photostat, microfilm, xerography, or any other means, or incorporated into any information retrieval system, electronic or mechanical, without the written permission of the copyright writer.

All inquirers should be addressed to:
Book Savvy International
1626 Clear View Drive, Beverly Hills California 90210, United States
Hotline: (213) 855-4299
https://booksavvyinternational.com/

Ordering Information:

Amount Deals. Special rebates are accessible on the amount bought by corporations, associations, and others. For points of interest, contact the distributor at the address above.

Printed in the United States of America.

ISBN-13	Paperback	978-1-958876-01-5
	eBook	978-1-958876-00-8
	Hardback	979-8-89190-207-7

Library of Congress Control Number: 2022912821

TABLE OF CONTENTS

CHAPTER ONE
THE MAINSTREAM GAME..1

CHAPTER TWO
THE WHAT AND WHY OF MAINSTREAM AMERICA........................7

CHAPTER THREE
THE WHITE MALE SUBURBAN RESERVATION..........................15

CHAPTER FOUR
LIFE OUTSIDE THE MAINSTREAM GAME................................23
MY FIRST ENTRY INTO THE CORPORATE MAINSTREAM..................28

CHAPTER FIVE
THE CHALLENGE OF LIVING IN TWO OR MORE CULTURES................31

CHAPTER SIX
THE STEPS TO MAINSTREAM FLUENCY..................................41

CHAPTER SEVEN
THE DYNAMICS OF STEREOTYPING OR BEING STEREOTYPED.............47

CHAPTER EIGHT
BRIDGING CULTURAL TRUST GAPS.....................................63

CHAPTER NINE
RACISM/SEXISM IN AMERICA..69

CHAPTER TEN
SHARING YOUR JOURNEY WITH OTHERS................................77

CHAPTER ELEVEN
THE DYNAMICS OF CULTURE..89

CHAPTER TWELVE
LOOKING BACK, GOING FORWARD: *THE AFRICAN-AMERICAN JOURNEY TO MAINSTREAM AMERICA*..101

CHAPTER THIRTEEN
WOMEN AND THEIR JOURNEY TO THE MOUNTAIN TOP..................111

CHAPTER FOURTEEN
THE RULES OF MAINSTREAM AMERICA: *THE "UNWRITTEN RULES" OF THE GAME*..121

CHAPTER FIFTEEN
THE POSITIVES AND NEGATIVES OF PLAYING THE GAME................129

CHAPTER SIXTEEN
MAKING THE BUSINESS CASE FOR TEACHING THE RULES................135

CHAPTER SEVENTEEN
　DECIDING IF THE JOURNEY IS RIGHT FOR YOU 143

CHAPTER EIGHTEEN
　CHARTING OUR PROGRESS 161

CHAPTER NINETEEN
　FINAL THOUGHTS ON WHAT LIES AHEAD 171

CHAPTER TWENTY
　IMPORTANT SKILLS TO CONSIDER ON YOUR JOURNEY 181

CHAPTER TWENTY-ONE
　THE DREAM I HAVE FOR AMERICA 193

CHAPTER ONE

THE MAINSTREAM GAME

Sometime in your working career, you might have been given some sage advice in the form of the statement, "Hey, you gotta play the game!" Even though that wise mentor might not have been able to define this "game" in much detail, they were right. There is a game that we are all in and if we choose to play, we will be playing by the rules that define "Mainstream America." These rules are defined by the power structure of our country and our organizations. These rules are also often "unwritten" but they form the acceptable codes of conduct, mores, and norms that define our society and its value systems. Because the rules are often not written down and are passed on to a limited population, I call it the "Best Kept Secret in America."

For those who have taken a stand by stating that "I don't play games" (which they have the perfect right to take that position); are merely saying I'm not following any rules but my own. However, this is a very risky position to take, since one of the cardinal unwritten rules is, "Whoever is at the top of a pyramid has the right to make the rules." (We will discuss this rule in detail later in this book). The risk is to suffer the consequences as we did when we chose not to play by the rules that were issued by our parents or our teachers in their classrooms. In my experience, it wasn't pretty.

LET'S LOOK AT LIFE AS BEING A "GAME"

I would like to propose that **LIFE IS A GAME**. As in every game, there have to be rules outlining the code of conduct that one has to follow and actions one has to consider if they want to win. The sharing of the rules is important because knowing the rules of any game allows all participants an equal chance of competing fairly and possibly winning. Rarely, if ever, will you find an accomplished player of any game, which is always competitive by definition, ignorant of the rules of the game in which he or she is playing. The same is true of the game of life. The comment, "you gotta play the game" is good and spot-on advice. Because these rules are not always shared with everyone. Let's take a moment to quickly put this "game" in perspective and take a brief look at the origin of our system. Later in Chapter thirteen, we will discuss specifically its rules and how the system works.

There actually is a game with a specific set of rules that keeps our society from cascading into chaos and anarchy. I outlined these rules in some depth in my first book, **Empowering Yourself: The Organizational Game Revealed,** and they will be summarized later in this book. The rules of this societal game fall into two categories - those rules that are "written" and those that are "unwritten." The written rules include the Federal, State, and Local laws that are passed by the various legislatures. These laws tell us what we can or cannot do and the penalties that might be assessed if one fails to comply. They also include the policies that are spelled out in a company's manager or employee manual. The by-laws of an organization would also fall into the category of written rules.

Written rules are usually clearly defined but they can often be misinterpreted by individuals. In this case, there is usually some mechanisms in place to have the rules challenged. This could be the court system with governments, or the Human Resource Department in organizations. Even at the local country club, an appeal might be made to the president or the board of governors on any given issue that might be in dispute.

The "unwritten rules" are not as easy to understand or interpret. They are made up of traditions, values, and opinions originating from one person or a few people at the top of an organization. The unwritten rules will often be explained as "that's just the way we do it around here." Unwritten rules are the guidelines that allow people to understand what is acceptable behavior, not only in any organization but are also the elements that govern every society. It even allows the global economic structure to exist. In our country, we sometimes refer to unwritten rules as whether an action or statement is or is not "politically correct." As we have seen many times recently in the news, to step outside of political correctness with even a single comment, can bring and has brought many successful careers to a screeching halt.

WHERE DID IT ALL BEGIN?

To understand the origin of the rules by which we are currently playing in our society, we must refer to that cardinal rule again. That rule states, **"Whoever is at the top of any pyramid, has the right (and responsibility) to make the rules for that pyramid."** This would include as I mentioned, parents in the home, a teacher in the classroom, the principal in the school, a general in the Army, and even the Pope in the Catholic Church. In organizations, that would include the head person such as the CEO but would also include the head of a staff of three in a department.

The rules that are in place in our country are also the same rules that hold the global economy together and they are over eight hundred years old. That time span would take us back to around 1215, the signing of the Magna Carta and the beginning of the British Empire.

It was stated in colonial times that "The sun never sat on the British Empire" and of course, the United States was one of her colonies. It was at that time, being on top of the global economy and thus the global pyramid, England began making the rules under which the world currently operates. It is no accident that we speak English in the United States but also every other major country such as Japan, India, and South Korea, teaches their children English. China recently decreed that every child from the third grade and for their entire formal education must take a minimum of one English course every year. China will eventually be the largest English-speaking country in the world. They have moved into the world economic game and understand that speaking English in the future will be a basic requirement for them to be successful. If China should become dominant in five or six generations, according to the rules, our future generations may be compelled to learn Chinese in order to survive as the Chinese are doing today.

The rules, however, are much broader than just language. How we socially interact as people also is an important factor in defining what rules are in play. This is an area where England has had an obvious influence. If you want to fit into the highest levels of any major society in the world, you will more than likely participate in several social activities. They include golf, which St. Andrews began six hundred years ago. Tennis, (which started over two hundred fifty years ago at Wimbledon), as well as sailing and yachting. (England is surrounded by water and was once a world sea power). Finally, this would include all activities surrounding the horse (polo, fox hunting, and horse racing). England refers to horse racing as the "sport of kings" and in the United States, we refer to that group of people as the "Horsey Set."

China is intensely addressing the game's rules. Since joining the global economy, they have built over five hundred golf courses and declared that in order to graduate from their three top universities, equivalent to our Harvard, Princeton, and Yale universities, you are required to take golf lessons. China is preparing its future workforce to be comfortable at the highest levels of the global economy when they begin their careers. They understand that there are rules in the global system and are ensuring that their young people are exposed to and are learning these rules.

WHAT THEN AGAIN IS MAINSTREAM AMERICA?

Knowing this helps us better to define what is mainstream America. It is simply the part of our society that plays by the rules that define the codes of conduct of our upper societal and organizational cultures. This includes people and organizations in the private sector, government, the military, non-profit, religious, and every other organization that falls under the rules set by the mainstream. These rules first emanated from English men who belonged to the Church of England. In our country, they were known as WASPs (White Anglo-Saxon Protestants).

It is important to note that every culture operates within its own pyramid and has cultures that have been defined by people at the top of that culture, sometimes many centuries ago. As an example, the Italian American culture can trace its beginnings back to the Roman Empire. Some of these ethnic, racial, and religious cultures would include Irish-American, Polish-American, Mexican-American, African-American, German-American, Jewish, Muslim cultures, and a long list of many others.

Of course, there are no right or wrong, good or bad cultures. All are rich in beautiful traditions, values, and codes of conduct. But because of our diverse American society and the diverse global economy, there has to be a common language or set of rules to enable effective communication between different groups and different nations. It is also important for business norms and personal social interactions to be understood by all participants. This common ground in our country is the rules of mainstream America. In the United States, embracing these common traditions and codes of conduct is said to be "playing the game."

CHAPTER TWO

THE WHAT AND WHY OF MAINSTREAM AMERICA

If anyone even thinks about taking the journey to "Mainstream America," two issues should be discussed. These issues are what specifically is mainstream America and why should one consider going there. To address the first issue as to what is Mainstream America, we must go back into our history. Although England was one of the first immigrant groups to settle in the land of our Indigenous American ancestors, America is a "melting pot," and it has been so from the very beginning. The melting might be a slow process but we are a melting pot nonetheless.

The year after the English landed at Plymouth Rock, their leaders John Carver and Miles Standish combined forces with the Pokanoket Native American tribe, under the leadership of Squanto. Together, the two groups shared knowledge, set rules and standards, and as a result, began a society that started the blending of cultures. In this case, it was a blending that allowed the new British colony to survive. The customs and rules they established were the beginning of the American mainstream.

Because we are a nation of immigrants, the groups of immigrants and the contributions they have made over our history are endless. Just a few include Africans, under enslaved immigration, who were the foundation of the cotton industry and the economy of the south. The Chinese and the Continental Railroad, the Irish and the Erie Canal, Native Americans building our skyscrapers, and Mexican Americans harvesting our food are a list that goes on and on.

As each immigrant group added itself to the melting pot, not only brought skills but also the richness of their cultures. This blending becomes the accepted code of conduct for our nation and a vehicle for all cultures to be able to communicate and work with each other. It is a false assumption that America's mainstream is a set of White "unwritten rules."

The reality is the mainstream has a little of all of us in it. It might appear that mainstream America consists of only the "white" culture simply for the fact that the first expansion of immigrants into our country mainly came from Europe and laid the foundation of our system based on their experiences and cultures.

Demographic predictions tell us that future immigration will be more representative of the entire world, not just Europe. The impact of these new cultures on our mainstream will take generations to have their impact, but it is inevitable that it will happen. We have seen it in the past with the Irish, Italian, Polish, German, and Greek cultures, and it will continue with the Asian, Hispanic, African, and Middle Eastern cultures entering our country in the future.

Therefore, when I suggest in this book that you might consider playing by the rules of the American "mainstream," I am not suggesting that you must think and/or act "White." My suggestion is that you might want to consider thinking and acting like an "American," which is made up of every race, religion, and ethnic group that exists in the world, and all are represented in the American culture. We are a nation of blended cultures. That's what we were in the very beginning with the British and the Pokanoket Native Americans and that's what it will be to the end of our existence.

Just as the first two cultures, by learning from each other and working together, made the first settlement succeed, so will this ability to blend cultures to become stronger define our future. Learning ways for the diverse workforce to grow as individuals and work together as teams will dictate the fate of all organizations as well as America on the future global stage.

LIVING ON OUR "RESERVATIONS"

There are many reasons why we will have difficult challenges in creating cooperative and productive future diverse teams. Key among these challenges are the many divisive elements that make up our nation. These divisions include such items as race, gender, sexual orientation, red and blue political philosophies, ethnic backgrounds, and socio-economic separations just to name a few. To add to the complexity of this multitude of differences is that we are very tribal. We love the comfort of being around our own.

Therefore, one of the biggest challenges we face is how to entice more people to consider leaving their physical and mental reservations. Let me explain what I mean by using the term "reservation."

Many of us have "reservations" in which we live. These reservations can be physical or geographical in nature such as those forced upon the Native American people at the turn of the twentieth century. But the other major reservations of which I speak are mainly mental in nature. These "Mental Reservations" are formed and defined by our own individual comfort zones which we have established for ourselves. The worlds outside of our mental reservations consist of unknown elements and environments that we have not experienced personally and fill us with feelings of discomfort and even a degree of fear. Even if those outside worlds are known, they are often considered hostile and can make people feel very unwanted.

However, within the reservations in which we all live, there is comfort, familiarity, and a warm sense of belonging. In our physical reservations, we are familiar with the culture, lifestyle, and values of our enclosed and restricted environments. In other words, we know the codes of conduct that are acceptable and those that are not. In knowing and understanding our reservation's rules, we can conduct ourselves in accordance with the personal goals we have set for ourselves and the life objectives we wish to pursue. One can quickly see how difficult it is for anyone to leave the comfort and safety of the world in which they grew up and/or are currently living.

Mental reservations are a part of everyone's psyche, with many having more than one. Reservations can be of race, religion, socio-economic level, ethnic group, occupation, power status, and many other worlds in which a person might live. This, by no means, indicates that "Physical Reservations" no longer exist because they do. The difference today is people are not forced by law to live on reservations as were our early Indigenous citizens.

If one chooses to live within various communities, they may well have chosen to voluntarily live on that reservation. This would include locations such as "Little Italy," "Chinatown," the Black, Hispanic, Irish, Jewish, Japanese, Puerto Rican, Korean, and the many other ethnic and religious communities that many people of a specific identifiable group might live.

There is, however, one "physical" and "mental" reservation that is often overlooked. That reservation is the white, suburban, country club communities that exist in our country. Just like folks that live in their ethnic or religious reservations, many white Americans have surrounded themselves with only their fellow white, suburban, and country club associates with which they are comfortable. Some of those people rarely venture outside of their known and comfortable worlds and many may live their entire life (with possibly the exception of eight hours of work) not venturing outside of their comfortable existence. We will discuss the white male suburban reservation in more detail in later chapters.

The "mental reservations" of which I speak are defined by the world in which a person lives outside of his or her job. It includes hobbies, social activities, social circles, acquaintances, and friends. When work is over, with whom do you have drinks, and whom do you invite to the Saturday night party at your home? All of these things will define the boundaries and scope of a person's mental world. A house can be purchased in any suburban mainstream community, but if that person's social life is totally immersed in their racial, ethnic, or religious circles, that individual might have left his or her "physical reservation" but could still be mentally encased in the world of their native culture.

ARE OUR RESERVATIONS A BAD THING?

What's wrong with living in worlds that allow a person to be comfortable and happy? Absolutely nothing! Growing up in a culture that has been defined by your ancestors can be a wonderful, stabilizing experience for anyone. In this "game of life" however, we all have choices. The choices we make concerning our lives should make us happy. I would then suggest that, if remaining on either the mental or physical reservation that you have chosen to live does not harm others and makes you happy, then that is more likely, a great choice for you. Maybe even more strongly stated, that very well might be the right choice for you. It will remain the right choice until you, and only you, decide it is not. Both sides of this issue were very clearly described in Lin-Manuel Maranda's musical **In the Heights**. In it, he describes the warmth that his community provided everyone but also the emotional struggles that many of the young people had in deciding to stay or leave.

It is only when, by living on our mental reservations, it keeps us from reaching our life objectives or prevents us from being effective in a rapidly changing world, should we start to seriously examine the right environment that will allow us to accomplish our individual life goals.

These issues will most likely arise when your work requires the need for greater personal interaction with the workforce's changing demographics. One of the most important factors to remember in "The Game" that we will be describing later in this book is that "The game is about PEOPLE and everything else is detail." This statement merely indicates that individuals cannot reach their life goals without the help of people. If you are an entrepreneur, it takes a person to give you business, it takes a person to give you loans for your own business, and it takes people to whom you must sell your products. If you were fortunate enough to be hired by a person and have landed in an organization; every raise, important assignment, or promotion must come from a person. Even when success happens, it takes people for those rewards to be appreciated and enjoyed. Let's face it, life cannot be lived and enjoyed without people. But the people who can make and will be making those decisions involving you and your future are changing. Many of your future bosses will be people that will be different from your culture no matter what that core culture may be.

Multi-cultural interactions will increasingly be required at all levels within our organizations to accomplish your future organizational objectives. For an upward-oriented career, the need to become comfortable with people in executive positions becomes critical. If your future career requires you to work with people from other countries, having to learn more about other cultures and become comfortable with them is something we must all accept. There will come a time in any upwardly oriented career and for anyone who wants to upgrade their current lifestyle when they will not be required to interact with people outside of their reservations or comfort zones.

Of course, this does not apply to someone working in a small business that has its location in, for example, the Mexican-American community that is serving only Mexican-American customers or clients. These individuals do not have to venture into unknown and uncomfortable worlds to provide for themselves or reach their current work objectives. Life and work objectives, however, can be in a constant state of change and when a person wants to reach higher objectives, they must then review if their current environment will allow them to reach those new updated goals and objectives. If it cannot, leaving your mental or physical reservations and joining the mainstream might be a good strategy to consider.

The major interruption of one's mental reservation (or comfort zones) comes when a person has to work for a large organization that has people from many racial, religious, and ethnic backgrounds. However, as I mentioned earlier, this is usually only for eight hours a day, five days a week, at work. After leaving that environment, most will quickly hurry back to the comfort of their reservations. These comfort zones may include hanging out with their neighbors, going to their clubs, their favorite bars, or any other place where they can meet with people just like themselves.

There are some good and some bad elements in this scenario. The good is that our reservations are available to us after a long hard day dealing with people who are not from our unique reservation. The bad is that since "the game is about people" and you rarely have a chance to get to know the people with whom you work, except on a surface basis; you become limited in your knowledge of people that are not living in the narrow or limited world you have chosen. This is what I am calling "mental reservations."

It is fair to ask the question, "Why is it important to get to know about people who make you uncomfortable?" That question gets us back to the world of reality. The Census Bureau predicts that by 2060 white males will represent only twenty-nine percent of the American workforce. That means that women and members of every ethnic, religious, and racial group will be needed to share power and make contributions to our society in addition to just the white male population. This is not an academic exercise but a reality. Those white males who choose to not come off their current "white male reservations" will not be very effective in managing, leading, and developing the future workforce of our country. In essence, those individuals who choose to remain on their ethnic, religious, and racial reservations may also not be effective in the world of the future. Add the fact that the world by 2060 will truly be a global economic environment, not being able to communicate effectively and be comfortable with people who are different from you, will place extreme limitations on any and all individuals who choose to stay in their self-imposed limited worlds.

CHAPTER THREE

THE WHITE MALE SUBURBAN RESERVATION

Before I begin this conversation, I'd like to say, "Some of my best friends are white guys." What I am about to share is in no way being critical of white males but merely reflects my observations and experiences. The suburban white male is the largest group in our country that operates in their "mental, cultural reservation."

That fact is difficult for many to understand because it is widely believed that once a white male leaves his ancestral physical reservation (which happens to many one or two generations after immigration), it is automatically assumed that they have reached mainstream America. That may not necessarily be the case. If you accept the definition that mainstream America is the historical blending of all of America's cultures, many white males exist totally in their comfortable world of socially staying in their "white only" world.

Of course, there is nothing wrong with anyone doing that, but it is no different from what we see being done in every culture. Simply leaving their ethnic cultural communities but joining the white male cultural group does not mean that they have joined "Mainstream America." There will be members of all cultural groups that will venture out of their exclusive ethnic, racial, or religious cultural worlds, and others in every cultural group that will remind mentally committed to only surrounding themselves "with their own kind."

SKIN COLOR: THE DIFFERENCE THAT MAKES A DIFFERENCE

The reason why white males make up the largest mentally and culturally restricted group is simply they (along with their significant others) make up the largest population in our country. There are several reasons why so many white males remain on mental, cultural reservations in our society, but a major one is our nation's reaction to skin color. Skin color is a difference that truly makes a difference in most societies. The reason skin color is so powerful in people's assessment and /or judgment of other people is, it is the first thing we see when any person comes into our view. Skin color also makes it easier for European ethnic groups to more quickly blend into the dominant white structure.

In our country, we all have been indoctrinated on the bias of skin color with white skin being the highest level of acceptability. In my childhood, I remember learning the jingle, "If you're white—you're alright, if you're brown—you can hang around, if you are yellow—you're mellow but if you're black—step back." Little did I know at the time, how that little jingle actually laid out the racial reality of our country.

In the twenties and thirties, as light-skinned "colored people" saw the advantages that white-skinned people had in our society, some tried to "pass" as being white. This was such an uncomfortable thing for white nightclubs to accept that many clubs would hire "spotters." They were black people, who could better spot another black person that was passing for being white than could white people and thus be able to block their entrance into those clubs. White skin color was the criteria for acceptance, even if most people could not detect the subtle differences in skin tone.

A great example that shows our society's reaction to skin tone can be found in the history of basketball and the NBA. As with most sports in our country, basketball was invented by a white man and only white men played it. However, by the early seventies, black players were starting to dominate the game both in skill and numbers. Some teams were even fielding all-black starting lineups. It had gotten to the point that attendance at the games had fallen off so much that many predicted that the league would not survive.

Then entered Larry Bird for the Boston Celtics and his skills and white skin was all that was needed to revive that sport at the professional level. He became "the great white hope" of basketball. Just the opportunity to see such a skilled white player among all the blacks who were playing was enough to turn basketball's attendance around. Of course, this scenario has been repeated often in sports including the coining of the term "the Great White Hope." It was the hope many Americans had in trying to find a white man that could defeat Jack Johnson, the Black Heavyweight boxing champion, at the start of the 19th Century. Of course, these actions can fall under the terms; racism, superiority, discrimination, and many others but one major factor in our decision-making about people will always be skin color. It is the one barometer that we can use to determine how we feel about a person before we meet them. We can spot skin tones from across a room.

If a person has not been sensitized to the power of skin color and the subconscious affect it has on all of us (both black or white), it often can prevent us from looking deeper into that individual. Of course, only if we can look beyond the surface of skin color, will we discover the true nature of that person. Beneath the color of one's skin, we can determine such important elements that define a person such as character, ethics, morals, level of their compassion and caring, sense of loyalty and trustworthiness, and the many other things that define who that person really is. It was Dr. Martin Luther King who wished for the day that we no longer would judge a person by the color of their skin but instead by the content of their character.

White males who have left their physical cultural reservations

Of course, most college-educated white males (and white women as well) have descended from their ancestral physical reservations which include such communities as Germantown, Little Italy, the Irish, Polish, Russian, and the many other communities first started by European immigrants. Many, if not most white people in our time, are 2nd, 3rd, and even more generations from their immigrant beginnings.

During this time period, many have altered their ethnic names and even disconnected themselves from their ethnic backgrounds by just thinking of themselves as not being Irish or German but just being "a white guy." By these actions, they are defining themselves as reaching mainstream America. However, by defining mainstream America as being white America, many white males have put themselves in cocoons and have blocked out the changes that are slowly happening in our country. Today, as many people of color enter into their 2nd and 3rd generation of living in the American mainstream, mainstream America is making a multi-cultural transition. It is slow, but there is a transition happening nonetheless.

This, of course, is not to imply that all suburban whites are racist. Many white males have openly embraced the multi-cultural changes that are taking place in our nation. However, at a white person's party on a Saturday night and there are no people of color attending, it is no different than an all-black party, an all-Asian party, a gay/lesbian party, an all-Jewish party, etc.; It's just not looked upon as a group that is clannish if it is an all-white party. An all-white Saturday party is considered the acceptable norm versus those other groups that will be labeled as just wanting to keep to themselves in their own little worlds. The reality is, white folks, want to be comfortable at Saturday night social functions just like every other group. But pressure is being applied to the white male power structure as more women and people of color are gaining power positions in our organizations.

Why is it so difficult for white males to leave their mental reservations?

The effort to leave the white male mental reservation is much more difficult for that group because they feel there is no pressing reason to do so. When connected to the power group, there is little need to move out of your comfort zone. However, this is rapidly changing. For a white male to not invite or socialize with their boss or bosses' boss because they are not like them can now be as politically damaging to their careers as it has been for members of minority communities who have practiced that avoidance policy for decades.

Looking to the future, several factors will come into play to help white males become more comfortable with diverse individuals. Those factors are:

We have already indicated how difficult it is to become comfortable with individuals if your only contact with them is on the job from 9 to 5. Conversations at work may be polite and even fun but the subject matter discussed is usually about very surface issues and rarely do they allow people to really get to know each other. As members of the minority communities begin to participate in activities of the white majority (such as playing golf, tennis, skiing, or sailing, these will act as bridges to more interactive activities and thus lead to more intimate conversations. It is much easier to invite a person of color who is on your tennis team to your party than it is to do so with someone with whom you work. The job just is not enough to establish personal bonds between individuals.

This is best illustrated when we look at the very deep bonds that happen on athletic teams. It was displayed by Gail Sayers/Brian Piccolo's friendship in the movie "Brian's Song." Maybe not all sports relationships end up with that deep of a bond but athletics who play on the same team for a number of years and experience the joys of victory and the agonies of defeat together, very often forge lifetime friendships. Even the most resistant members of the Brooklyn Dodgers eventually became great friends and supporters of Jackie Robinson.

Getting comfortable with people who are different from you is not an easy thing to do. It usually is done only when one is forced into that situation. We have seen this in the diversification of our workplaces, our schools, our neighborhoods, and even our families. Many people can embrace people of differences until a family member marries someone outside of the family's race or religion. That reluctance to accept however, often starts to wain when the first baby is born to that couple. There is nothing that allows a family to accept differences more than a new baby.

It will be easier for individuals to accept people of a different race when it becomes less acceptable not to do so. What is currently making this easier is the number of mixed-race commercials that we are all currently seeing on television. What may have been shocking to many in the past is now so commonplace that we rarely take notice today. As time goes by, it will not be something that is thought about by most. Even though a person may not know a mixed couple in their personal life, it is coming into all of our living rooms via our televisions on a daily basis today.

BACK TO MAINSTREAM AMERICA

As mentioned before, many might assume that my reference to mainstream America is defining the rules of white America. It is worthy of repetition, I am not. The American melting pot is like chop suey or a stew containing a lot of different ingredients that come together to make a great dish. English men might have had a significant role in starting the American mainstream but as we all know from our history, German, Irish, Italians, and many other European ethnic groups quickly added to the American melting pot, each making significant contributions. Later adding to those contributions, as mentioned before, were formerly freed slaves, women, immigrants from Asia, the islands, and Hispanic nations. Mainstream America is a central place where anyone from any cultural group, can go to achieve the "American Dream."

Remember that cardinal rule in our system I mentioned before that states, "If whoever is at the top of a pyramid has the right and responsibility to make the rules, then it just so happened that the European settlers, dominated by the English, became the power base that established our first rules." There is nothing we can do to reverse history, it's just fact. But we also see in our history how the rules slowly have changed when more immigrants enter the American mainstream bringing with them new innovations, different prospective, talent, industry, enthusiasm, and most importantly, new standards of fair play. This process of very slow inclusion was also the start of the slow changing of the system's rules.

To do so, however, the new immigrants had to ascend to the top or at a minimum, be of influence with those individuals in rule-making positions. This is why sharing the knowledge of how our system works becomes most important. Sharing this knowledge with all groups will determine how long it will take for the top leaders of our system (government, business, religion, education, and family) to hear those new voices and perspectives and then be convinced that change should happen. Of course, in time those immigrants or their descendants will be in those decision-making positions themselves.

The latest additions to our nation and our workforce are taking more time to mainstream for several reasons. The major two are: the reluctance of the mainstream population in accepting or sponsoring the new entries into their tight and sometimes exclusive reservations that they have made for themselves, and the reluctance of the new entries to jump into the unknowns of the mainstream. However, even if slow, it is this blending of all of our races and cultures that give the American Mainstream its richness and strength.

THE PRICE OF TRYING TO CHANGE THE MAINSTREAM

This richness and strength, however, usually come at a price. Our history has shown that most of our major changes have come after there were protests, demonstrations, and unfortunately, sometimes violent activity. This can be seen in women gaining the right to vote, the protest and strikes of unions to gain fair wages and working conditions, the demonstrations of Black Americans to gain the Civil Rights and Voting Rights Acts, the demonstrations that helped to end the Vietnam War, demonstrations of people with different sexual orientations gaining Gay Rights. The jury is still out as to the gains that may be won with such current movements as "Me Too" and "Black Lives Matter." All are looking to further the cause of equal justice and equality for all. Our history teaches us that even the beginning of our nation started with the protests, demonstrations, and even riotous actions from our Founding Fathers such as the Boston Tea Party. Their final violent course of action was resorting to war.

Of course, one of the greatest changes in our nation was the most violent. It took the Civil War and 655,000 people to die to free enslaved people. When living by the rule, "If it ain't broke why fix it," we have seen in our history that it usually takes protests and demonstrations to tell the power structure that something is broken and needs to be fixed.

Sharing our "mainstream" rules is most important to our nation's future success because in organizations where people interact daily, it will provide a neutral and common language for all who want to venture out from their self-imposed, comfortable reservations. Since our future workforce will consist of more women, people of color, and immigrants, this common language will be most valuable. In the future competitive global game, it will also give us a much more effective workforce that will be comfortable dealing with people from other countries and cultures. When we start to mentor and sponsor a much more diverse population into the mainstream system, we are, in essence, preparing our country for success in a future global economy, developing our workforce's future leaders as well as creating a more team-oriented environment.

This can only be done if we choose to share what the mainstream rules are and explain to our workforce how our system works. There is no doubt that our fiercely competitive global competitors are teaching their employees and children the "mainstream" business rules. Except for a very selective group of our young people, mainly those attending boarding and prep schools, we as a society are not. It is something I strongly feel we will regret. We cannot remain competitive with only such a small percentage of our future population being exposed to and instructed on mainstream rules. It is very much like us, as a nation, not preparing for our two World Wars when deep down inside, we knew they were eventually going to happen. Having our troops train with wooden toy guns did not fair well for us at the start of those wars. Not equipping all of our children with this valuable knowledge is reflective of our short-sightedness in training with wooden toy guns and thinking that it would be adequate for those impending conflicts.

CHAPTER FOUR

LIFE OUTSIDE THE MAINSTREAM GAME

A LITTLE ABOUT MY JOURNEY

Often, I have been asked how could a Black man be someone who would accurately figure out the rules that govern mainstream America. I can only relate it to the fact that I was an observer of the system when I was young and was not allowed to be a player. It was like not being a fish in a fishbowl struggling with the daily challenges and dynamics of aquarium life, but by being outside the fish bowl, I was able to observe all of the action without the emotions of competing with the requirements of the aquarium environment.

That was the situation in which I found myself growing up. I grew up in the forties and fifties in our country during the "Jim Crow" era. Those times were pretty rough for a "Colored" person. We are now all familiar with what we know as "the talk" that exists in the Black community. For those not familiar, it is the conversation that a parent of a Black son has at driving age, giving him the "Do's" and "Don'ts" after being stopped by a police officer. But that was the second talk I had with my father. My first "talk" was in 1949 when he explained that "when a White man approached me on a sidewalk, I should move to the side and never look him directly in the eyes." I had my second "talk" that dealt with driving when I turned sixteen.

In my hometown, Thursdays were "Colored night" at the local skating rink and Fridays were "Colored day" at the community swimming pool. I had to sit in the balcony at the local theater and could not sit at the counter in certain restaurants. I was truly outside of the game and became an outside observer.

Coming from a working-class family, it was understood that I had the responsibility to find work to help with my financial needs. Those jobs included picking fruits and vegetables on farms, working on a garbage truck, washing dishes in a restaurant, and cleaning ashes out of industrial furnaces. I was a shoeshine boy, a delivery boy, mowed lawns, a paper boy, and worked in a steel mill. However, there were some jobs that put me in contact with the country club set and allowed me to observe life and the code of conduct of the upper middle class.

I was employed at a country club as a caddy, a shoeshine boy, a men's locker room attendant, and a bus boy. In those positions, I was exposed to the games and activities that were being played by that group. Of course, as a caddy, it enabled me to learn the rules of golf and the courtesies that had to be displayed to be acceptable to that group. It also showed me the various emotions of the different golfers and which reactions to the game were acceptable and which were not. I saw who would not play by the rules of golf when no one but me was watching and those players who played the game with a strict ethical code.

As a locker room attendant, I learned all of the card games and the relationships that existed among the members according to their status. I was also privy to all of the business conversations and the political scheming that occurred. The busboy position exposed me to formal table settings, gourmet foods, and dinner conversations. I did not know it at the time nor did I appreciate the fact that I was getting a finishing school education. For me at that time, it was just work that was keeping me from doing fun things with my friends.

MY INTRODUCTION TO MAINSTREAM AMERICA

Anyone's first formal introduction to mainstream America is usually memorable. After all, you are stepping into a new world that you have only known from magazines, television, or movies. My introduction took place in New Castle, Pennsylvania, a small town near Pittsburgh, and it was a particularly dramatic one. It happened in 1946 when I was six years old. My family had just bought a house in a White neighborhood, the first Negro family to do so. It was a house located two doors from a large Methodist church. The first night as it was getting dark, I saw what I thought was a fire in the front yard. When I went to the window, I was amazed at the beautiful cross that was burning. Being two doors from the church I thought it was a "welcome to the neighborhood" gesture on behalf of the church members. I excitedly ran into the kitchen to tell my mother and father of the nice gift we had just been given.

You can imagine my confusion when my father went to the window and my always calm mother was screaming for my father to step away. I had never seen her so overcome with fear so I quickly got caught up in the emotion of the situation. I dropped to the floor and started pulling at my father's leg begging him to step away. Next came one of those life-changing moments you always remember. With the reflection of the flames of the burning cross on his face, my father stood tall at the window. He then looked down at me and said, "Harvey, never let anyone keep you from doing what you have a right and want to do." That experience and message have helped me many times on my mainstream journey, including the times when two other houses had burning crosses on the lawns that I bought later in my life.

LIVING IN A SEPARATE BUT UNEQUAL SOCIETY

The morning after the cross burning, my parents walked me and my two brothers to our new school. That was a task that would have been relegated to my mother but my father accompanied us as well. After the incident of that last evening, I remembered how comforting it was that I had the protection of both. Not knowing what to expect, I was quite surprised at the lack of incidents that occurred. I was introduced to my teacher, assigned a seat, and settled into my mainstream life. Children do adapt quickly to new environments and I was no exception. Fortunately, I was in the first grade, and children at that age do not carry with them deep lessons of prejudices. My two older brothers that were enrolled that day said they heard the "N" word but that was the extent of the racial drama for me and my family.

Things settled down quickly in my new neighborhood with me playing ball, cowboys, and war with the other neighborhood kids. It was not long before I even took the role of the leading cowboy and not the sidekick. My mother also soon developed relationships with our neighbors. Those relationships grew for thirty years, with many of those neighbors eventually becoming my mother's best friends.

CROSS BURNINGS REVISITED

A similar thing happened with my second cross-burning experience. It was in Princeton Junction, New Jersey (a suburb of Princeton). Little did I know that at the time, it was six miles from the Northeastern headquarters of the Ku Klux Klan. The first night we were awakened to another six-foot burning cross. It was much more emotional than the first cross-burning experience I had earlier in my life because this time I had two children and of course, was worried about their welfare. I got through it all remembering what my father had said to me when I was six, "Don't ever let anyone keep you from doing what you have the right and want to do." We as a family stuck it out and just like in my neighborhood growing up, my neighbors in Princeton became good social friends. I do have to admit, however, that at the Friday night neighborhood parties, I would often wonder if any of my neighbors had a hand in the cross burning. After the initial "I'm sorry that happened" from everyone in the neighborhood, no one ever discussed it again.

During those Jim Crow times, I became very active. I was arrested twice at sit-ins, was at Dr. King's "I have a dream" speech, was a Mississippi freedom rider, and had the opportunity to train Andy Young's staff when he was Mayor of Atlanta. I also had the honor of being one of seven people who attended the first two meetings with Coretta King when she began her plans to build the King Center.

A MISSISSIPPI FREEDOM RIDER

There is a back story behind the Mississippi freedom ride. It was when I was living in Princeton Junction at the time and was going to catch our Freedom Bus leaving from Philadelphia. My daughter was expected to be born the day the bus was scheduled to leave and of course, I had to cancel. I did pledge that if she came early, I would catch a plane and meet the group. She was born early on the day that the bus was scheduled to depart. After having such a short bonding time with my wife and new daughter, I, of course, was very reluctant to leave. When I told Kita (my wife) of my reluctance, she gave me the courage I needed to go by simply looking at my new daughter Kellie and saying, "Don't feel bad, you're not doing it for yourself, you're doing it for her." I caught a plane to Memphis and rented a car for the drive to Itta Bena, Mississippi. By the time I got near Philadelphia County, (the place where the three earlier freedom riders were murdered), it was 2:00 in the morning, pitch dark with no signs of lights or of life.

When I saw headlights in my rearview mirror, I thought little of it until suddenly the flashing lights of a police car made my heart jump into my throat. Remembering where I was, I didn't want to pull over but knew not doing so could prove fatal. It was not long before the two officers had me spread-eagled on the hood of my rental car and after some brief questioning, I heard one of the officers ask the other, "What do you think we should do?" The only thing that went through my mind was at least once I had a chance to hold my new baby daughter in my arms earlier that morning. They kept asking me about what school I was attending and I realized they were particularly looking for disruptive college students. I convinced them I was with IBM and was down merely for business. They let me go with a warning that I should pick my business locations a little more carefully and that it was dangerous for a Yankee to be down there. In essence, they were telling me to get out and not to come back. I have often thought that I am alive today because of the powerful reputation that IBM had at the time and the fact that I was wearing a suit. From that time until today, I have always embraced the power that business dress has on situations and people's attitudes.

GROWING UP LIVING IN TWO CULTURES

Growing up in those "separate but equal" times, however, did not keep me from having some fun. Although living just two doors from a large church that sponsored a Boy Scout troop that all my neighborhood friends belonged to, I was not allowed to join. Wanting to be a Boy Scout, I joined the "Colored" troop that was in the colored community. I had an amazing time and an unforgettable learning experience. I am still very proud that I am an Eagle Scout, the first Negro in my county at the time to achieve that goal. I have often wondered how much of my motivation to work so hard at accomplishing that honor came from trying to show my white friends in my neighborhood that I could do it without their white troop.

One of the most fun experiences that I had in my youth was when I and a group of my friends went into the boy's room at our high school and began to sing a song that was on the current "Hit Parade." We thought we sounded pretty good and decided to form a "Du-wop" group. With much practice and determination, we did become good enough to open for many groups in the Pittsburgh area on what was then called the "Chitlin' Circuit."

Some of those artists included James Brown, Ray Charles, Little Anthony, and the Imperials, Bobby Darin, and others.

MY FIRST ENTRY INTO THE CORPORATE MAINSTREAM

THE ERA OF "THE FIRST"

After the 1964 Civil Rights Act was passed, it unlocked the mainstream door for women and people of color in our country. It opened the playing field for all Americans to be able to compete in the game that had previously only been available to White males. As a result, these new entries into the workforce had a chance to accomplish many things that became the first for that particular group. It was not only a sense of pride to hear that a member of your group had gained a milestone for your race or gender, but it was also very motivational. You thought, as an example in my case, if one Black person can do that, why don't I try?

One of my initial career "firsts" came when I was looking for career choices the last few months before I graduated from college. It came about by pure accident. I was looking at the University Placement manual that had pages of corporations listing their benefits for students and why they should apply to their respective companies. I came across Xerox Corporation's ad that was very simple but stopped me in my tracks. I can still remember it after over fifty-five years. It was a full eight by eleven page with a totally gray background. On the page was simply the company's name in the lower right corner and in the middle with bold white letters "WE ARE AN EQUAL OPPORTUNITY EMPLOYER." I wasn't sure what that really meant at that time or even what Xerox did as a corporation, but it seemed that they might be asking me to apply, which I did. It took a while but after seven different interviews in three different locations, I was hired by Xerox as their first Black salesman.

Black publications at the time like Jet and Ebony Magazines and later Black Enterprise would always keep us apprised of the new barriers that were being broken by other Blacks all over the country. I have since realized that there was also a negative factor in hearing about all of "the firsts" that were happening in any given organization. Clearly, it was motivational hearing of all of the accomplishments that Blacks were making in our society, but it often became a competitive goal to compete with other Blacks to be the first of your group and not focus on mainstream competitors by instead, trying to be the "best" and not just the first.

In today's work environment, many if not most positions have checked off the "First Black" title for most career positions. Even the job of President of the United States can no longer be a first for an African American or the Vice President position as well. With that Vice President position, firsts were also broken for women and people of Indian ancestry. This is not true with many other minority groups. There are still challenges ahead for many current American communities, but every year these "first" career positions are becoming less and less for all groups. For example, today it is very difficult for a woman to say "They will never make a Woman chairman of the board." That might be true at any given company but women have made it to that position in many major companies. As a matter of fact, the two corporations with whom I used to work, Xerox and IBM, both have had women Chairman (Chairperson), with Xerox appointing an African American woman to that position. We recently received the first Native American woman appointed to a Presidential Cabinet position. The pot is continuing its melting process but now at higher levels.

And so, now with the playing field becoming a little more level, and Equal Opportunity no longer having the critical emphasis it had in the sixties and seventies, the best tool that any American worker can have today is knowledge of the rules of the American game so that they can play this game to the best of their individual ability. I must stress the word "individual" because when considering joining the American mainstream, it cannot be done as a group. It is a decision a person can only make for him or herself. Taking along a large group of family members and friends is not an option. Unfortunately, in these situations, you must often leave behind all who do not choose to join you on your journey.

CHAPTER FIVE

THE CHALLENGE OF LIVING IN TWO OR MORE CULTURES

Learning the difficult and often stressful situations that must be endured that are associated with living in two cultures, is something that everyone experiences when one ventures into mainstream America. This is why, when any group immigrates to our country and the numbers can justify it, they usually move into a community with people with whom they are comfortable and with whom they can effectively communicate. Thus, we see in almost every major coastal city, neighborhoods with names like Little Italy, Germantown, China Town, and communities that were inhabited by the Japanese, Cubans, Mexicans, Blacks, Jewish, etc.

Many of those people will never have to experience what it is like to live a dual life because they will never leave their community. This is a good thing because the richness that exists in the mainstream is due to those who remain in their communities and thus keep generating the artistic and cultural creations that constantly add to the richness of our country. It is usually the 2nd generation when their children attend schools and are exposed to mainstream children, that those children start to learn mainstream rules.

However, at the same time, they bring with them values and elements of their culture that influences the children of mainstream America. It is truly a two-way exchange. For these emerging children, it often becomes a balancing act that can be very stressful for all sides. In my case, I can remember when the best friend I had just made at school asked if I would come over for an after-school visit to see his new train set. We were stopped at the door by his mother and told that I couldn't come inside.

LEARNING A DIFFERENT CULTURE

Learning another culture is very much like learning a foreign language. It might take a lifetime or it can be done in a very short time period depending on the motivation and urgency one has to do so. For example, if you go to work in France with no knowledge of French and all you have is a book for translation, for the first few months you will spend much of your time frantically looking up words to just survive. However, after six months you will have learned basic words and even phrases that you can repeat from memory. In a year you might be able to put short sentences together that soon will grow into paragraphs. If you stay involved, in two to three years you might be able to think of concepts and subconsciously have enough command of French to explain those concepts without having to consciously think of the words. This is called becoming fluent in that language.

We see this happening with immigrants in our country all the time. We also see that it is entirely possible to speak fluently in many languages. For example, in Europe, because of the close proximity of countries, many people become fluent in multiple languages. The same rules apply to learning about other cultures. However, when two people of different cultures meet for the first time in business and don't have time to learn about each other's culture, their differences, however, can be bridged by simply communicating in the mainstream business culture.

Many people feel that if they become comfortable with another culture, they are selling out their native culture. But just as it is possible to learn several other languages, as many people do, and not forget their native language, so it is possible to learn multiple cultures without "forgetting where you came from." Learning about other cultures just makes you more effective with more people. And, as mentioned before, this game of life is about people, everything else details.

WHY MUST WE HAVE TO HAVE RULES?

Having pride in your cultural background is not unique to any one race or ethnic group, but all have had to leave behind many of their cultural comforts when they entered mainstream America. The first or second-generation Italian American who moved out of "Little Italy" must leave that environment with all of its rich culture when they move into the entry levels of large organizations. A person who has parents that still live in Chinatown, the Korean, Irish or German communities, all experience a sense of loss and an abandonment of their culture when they break from their perspective communities. A good comparison would be the feeling we all had when we first left our family home. It might have been to go to college, join the military, or take a job in another town. No matter the reason, it was something we knew had to be done but for many, it was not easy.

This transition to the mainstream way of living, of course, becomes easier with the greater number of generations that have passed since leaving their cultural communities. As an African-American, I often hear from members of my race that feel we are the only ones in the game that have to give up elements of our culture. This is just not true. Many of the earlier immigrants into our system even went so far as to change their family names to become more mainstream.

Another interesting observation is, once anyone leaves their level three (working class) communities, they are no longer referred to by their rich cultural backgrounds such as Italian, Polish, German, etc., But are simply referred to, as I have mentioned before, as just being White. I have never heard anyone who was referred to as a "white guy" make the correction that "No I am not, I'm really Italian." Of course, they have pride in their background but don't feel the need to be totally defined by it. This is a major step that must be addressed in reaching mainstream America.

WHOSE SIDE ARE YOU ON, ANYWAY?

One of the greatest challenges in living in two cultures is the stress and pressure of having to answer the hypothetical question, "Whose team are you on anyway?" Unfortunately, there are some that have such a great sense of pride and loyalty to their racial, religious, cultural traditions, customs, and values that they often demand of their friends that everyone must openly decide and display which culture is most important to them. For those individuals, they think there should be no fence-sitting. It is, are you with our culture or the mainstream culture? The more basic question that is really being asked is, "Are you with them or with us?"

The reason for many people wanting an answer to that question is simply, since the person to whom the question is being asked, is acting more like "those people" than he does us; it is assumed that he has turned his back on his own people. With that conclusion, someone can very easily be labeled as a "sell-out." Other labels include Uncle Tom, Oreo (for Blacks), and Banana (for Asians) as examples. These labels are extremely hurtful for any person who is just trying to balance their two worlds. In most cases, these two worlds include their world at work and their world of family and friends that emanates from their ethnic, religious, or racial reservations.

That was my experience when I grew up in my small town as a Black American and lived in a White neighborhood. I attended an all-White school but still socially lived in the Black community. Of course, I didn't go to the White Methodist church that was two doors away but instead, attended our Black AME (African Methodist Episcopal) church across town. Also, I was only allowed to attend the Black YMCA, had a Black-only scout troop, dated only "Colored" girls (one of the joys of my youth) and of course, lived with and enjoyed my Black family. The "them or us" world that I was told to live, did not affect the fun and great memories I have of my youth. The positive effect that it had on my life was, it forced me to become multi-cultural, a comfort that has helped me exist better in a multicultural world.

Sports was usually the only time when my two worlds collided. When white kids from my neighborhood competed with the black kids across town, which often put me in the role of mediator or peacemaker between the groups. I was constantly trying to explain that, "He didn't really mean anything by that" or "He really is a nice guy." Sometimes it worked, sometimes it didn't.

However, each time I stepped in to defend or justify the actions of any individual no matter what side they were on, members of the other side had reason to question my loyalty to them.

GETTING BEYOND THE LABELS WE MUST WEAR

But this neutral stance often labeled me as a sell-out or prompted a comment like, "You think you're White don't you" from my Black friends. Seventy years later, I see this dynamic still existing in the organizational world. It is not as openly stated as back in the fifties and sixties, but the underlining feeling of many people is that you cannot live in two worlds and that you must choose where your loyalty lies. When it is seen that a person is trying to learn another culture, the "selling out" comment is one of the most effective ways to keep, as we often say, the crabs in the barrel. After all, who wants to deny the culture of their family and friends? Couple this with not being sure the mainstream world will even accept you, the decision might well be, just stay at home where you belong.

The core reason that this occurs so often might be the fear of change. You are being confronted with the need to break away from the comfortable actions you have practiced all of your life. The new requirements will be different for you and with your lack of fluency in the mainstream language you might even resent having been made to communicate through the language of the business culture.

GOING MAINSTREAM VERSUS FORSAKING CULTURE

This is the most difficult conflict to resolve. I know it was for me and so many other of my friends growing up. However, as I grew older and started to better understand the rules, they started to make more sense. My greatest discovery was that everyone who wanted the things I wanted at the level I wanted them, had to do things I was reluctant to do. Remembering the rule that "Whoever is at the top of any pyramid has the right to make the rules," I started to realize that I was limited by the various "reservations" that I had defined for myself and started to observe that the game's rules truly did apply to everyone and that meant for me as well.

I slowly began to realize that I was not going to be the exception to those rules. If you don't think that England's social activities haven't expanded to the entire world, just watch the U.S. golf or tennis Open. Every major nation will have players that will be participating. This just shows that the game is global and that there are specific activities that anyone can learn to connect to a language that is spoken around the world.

Many times, when I suggest to People of Color the benefits of learning how to play golf, or tennis or learn about opera or ballet, their response is often "Why do I have to learn all of those white interests and activities to be successful?" Being a very proud African-American, I often remind them of the contributions that African-Americans have made to all of those "White" activities. In Opera, stars such as Paul Robeson, and Marion Anderson were not only great opera singers but were great contributors to the advancement of civil rights. Later opera singers such as Leontyne Price and Jesse Norman are more current opera legends. At one time, I read that the New York Metropolitan Opera, considered by many to be the greatest opera company in the world, had African-Americans as seventeen of their top principal singers.

In motion pictures, pioneers like Sidney Poitier not only set a standard of excellence in that art form but also created roles that change the nation's stereotypical opinions as to how African-Americans were viewed in real life. In the roles he played in the movies "Lilies in the Field," "In the Heat of the Night," "To Sir with Love," and "Guess Who's Coming to Dinner" directly addressed the issues of race relations, prejudice, and stereotyping.

In tennis, Althea Gibson and Arthur Ashe were past superstars and today Venus and Serena Williams have set records that may never be equaled. Moving on to golf, all that has to be said is Tiger Woods. As for ballet, companies such as the Harlem Ballet Company and Alvin Ailey are considered some of the best in the world. Misty Copeland, the Prima Ballerina of the American Ballet Theatre, considered one of the best in the country, is African-American.

Now include Hispanic contributors such as Placido Domingo, and Jose Carreras in opera; Chi Chi Rodriguez, and Lee Trevino in golf; Rafael Nadal in tennis; Len Manual-Miranda in Broadway; the list becomes endless as to the changes and contributions women and people of color have had in influencing the rules. If you add the Asian culture which includes such legends as Yo-Yo Ma, all cultures have made numerous contributions to the arts. The younger generation of Asians are making an impact on all sports including both golf and tennis.

When you then consider the African-American past leaders of our nation, from Fredrick Douglas and Harriet Tubman, to more recent game changers such as Martin Luther King, Andy Young, Colin Powell, Condoleezza Rice, President Obama, our current Vice President, Kamala Harris, newly appointed Supreme Court Justice Ketanji Brown Jackson and the recently numerous appointed multi-cultural presidential cabinet members, the rule-makers in our country are truly changing. To be more specific, fifty percent of the current President's Cabinet consists of women, and fifty percent of the positions are filled with people of color. Represented in the current cabinet are African-Americans, Hispanic-Americans, an Asian American, a Native American, an Immigrant and a Gay American.

If you buy into the unwritten rule that people at the top of any pyramid makes the rules, we must now consider the rules that are being made has to be "Mainstream American" rules. Our rules are now being made by members of every major cultural group in our country. To deny the many contributions that people of color, women, immigrants, and people of sexual differences have made and are currently making is denying reality and our true history.

With the head of our delegation to the United Nations, the head of the powerful Environmental Protection Agency, two Supreme Court Justices being African-American, one Hispanic-American and four Women, the areas of Defense, Education, Housing, Trade, Finance, Health and Human Services, Small Business Administration, Science and Technology policy, Energy, Commerce, the Interior, National Intelligence, the head of Management and Budgets, all being run by women and people of color at the national level; it is hard to argue that the rules of our system are in the hands of only white males. We can no longer call the rules we play by a white man's game being played under "white man's rules."

The point is, a person might be limiting themselves as well as diminishing the great contributions of African-Americans and other cultural groups if they categorize activities as being Black or White. If individuals are willing to expand their minds and become familiar with some of these accomplishments, they also can expand the possibilities of moving their life and career into upper-level positions.

The two factors that will control that possibility are the desire to want to aspire to those positions and the willingness to pay the dues of learning about the world in which those positions operate. Then, the only remaining challenge is to garnish the courage to try new adventures. Doing so just might change your life. The one thing that I can almost guarantee is that learning any of those sporting and artistic activities, will not make you less Black or any other racial, religious or cultural group. All of these individuals are people who are making policy and the rules not just for their race and gender but also for our nation and the entire world.

BEING YOUR AUTHENTIC SELF

One frequently voiced concern of young African-Americans today is the issue of wanting to be their "Authentic Self." In addressing the authentic self-issue, it is very difficult to give advice.

Since every individual must come up with their own definition of what their authentic self should be, it falls on all of our individual shoulders to make those decisions. It should be noted, however, that most people's definition of their authentic self could change many times in their lifetime. We were all our authentic selves in High School, but that definition may have changed by the time we graduated from college and even more so when and if we got married and started a family. To define who we are at one point in our lives and not redefine ourselves after many life experiences could be like having your feet stuck in a bucket of cement. Life can easily slip by without you realizing it happening. Again, the rule of when you're through changing, you may no longer be a serious competitor for upper-level positions, might be applied to this situation.

A serious self-examination on this issue should be made to ensure that wanting to remain your authentic self is not just wanting to go through personal change. It might also be a statement that you want to play by just your own set of rules. If that is the case, there might be major conflicts with the people who are at the top of your pyramids and who are making the rules to which they have the right. Remember when we were defining our authentic selves growing up in our parent's home and were quickly reminded "as long as you live under my roof." We learned then that the definition of who we are and how we should be able to conduct ourselves could be quickly altered for survival purposes.

THE SIX STEPS TO MAINSTREAM AMERICA FOR ALL CULTURES

One of the observations I have made about the journey that all cultures make to mainstream America comes in six steps. Those six steps are:

Step one: To collect themselves in a "Physical Cultural Reservation," much like our Native Americans who were forced to do so, every immigrant group does so voluntarily, (i.e., Little Italy, Germantown, the Irish, Jewish, Cuban, African-American, Chinatown, and the list goes on).

Step two: The children of immigrants start attending Mainstream American schools. They, of course, start to impact the schools with the richness of their cultures as well as bringing elements of the American mainstream culture back to their families and community.

Step three: Members from the various "Cultural Reservations" start to work in Mainstream American corporations and other organizations. By working with people of all cultures, they begin to learn the neutral culture of the mainstream that allows all of our cultures to communicate and work effectively together.

Step four: Members from the cultural reservations start to buy homes in suburban America. This is an indication that they not only have the means but also the desire to do so. However, most who do so still remain in what I call a "Mental, Cultural Reservation." This is displayed by still only socializing with their cultural group. As an example, their Saturday night party will only have members of their cultural group attending. It is important to note that the largest "mental, cultural reservation" we have in" this country is the one formed by the white suburban male. The impact on this group is, as the workforce becomes more multi-cultural and we become more global, many in this group are not preparing themselves to be leaders in a multicultural world.

Step five: Members of those cultural groups begin to expand their social life to include people of other cultures. This not only applies to cultures of color but also such cultures as the Jewish, Muslim, and communities representing sexual differences.

Step six: Members of those cultural groups begin learning the activities and lifestyle events of upper socioeconomic levels that represent the jobs they are seeking. This as an example, can be a working-class individual leaving their bowling league to join a golf league or expanding their music interest from rap or country music to include Broadway or symphonic music. It could also be a mid-level manager becoming interested in sailing or ballet. Learning these new activities is preparing them to be able to interface with people that their future jobs will require of them.

CHAPTER SIX

THE STEPS TO MAINSTREAM FLUENCY

BEING COMFORTABLE WITH AND ACCEPTING OTHER CULTURES

Becoming fluent in mainstream America should not be like jumping into the deep end of a swimming pool. A safer or more realistic strategy would be to first put your feet in, wade out to your waist, and then, only when you get comfortable and used to the water, would you completely submerge yourself. If you add to this scenario the fact that jumping into mainstream America is not like jumping into a stagnant pool but instead more like jumping into a fast-moving river. To make the plunge into either that river or mainstream America takes quite a bit more thought and I dare say courage.

The first toe in the water for most Americans usually happens with your job. If you have a job that isn't in your ethnic or racial community, you are most likely working in an environment that requires you to work with people of other cultures. If this is the case, your work culture will be governed by mainstream rules. After working with people of difference for a few years, people may develop relationships and become comfortable with each other to the point of even going out to lunch together. Members of work teams may then start to identify common interests such as the relationship they have with their boss or the mission and objectives of their department. This can even move to the level of talking about and understanding the common concerns they may have with family and other life situations.

Normally, however, this relationship is within the boundaries of the nine to five-time period that they work together. At five o'clock, everyone on the team will depart for their respective families, neighborhoods, and possibly their reservations. These relationships, however, can become close enough for people to make the comment. "Some of my best friends are (fill in the group)" or "I work with many of those people every day and have no problem with them." Of course, both statements are true but might not tell the complete story as to the true level of interaction with his or her "friend's" cultural, racial, or religious group.

GAUGING YOUR OWN LEVEL OF CULTURAL ACCEPTANCE

One of the easiest and often quoted statements that we make in our country is "I'm not prejudiced." When stated, it is often believed by the person making that claim. This can be said in confidence by that individual simply because of the contact they might have with people of other cultures. However, if we examine that statement in a little more detail, we see that there might be some flaws in it. This is because not being prejudiced has a lot to do with the environment in which one connects with people of another culture.

Let's look at the various levels or steps of involvement on the prejudice ladder and you can make a personal assessment of where you might be. Remember the word prejudice simply means that a person makes an assessment of an individual even before they know them. They pre-judge that person without any facts.

Step or Level One–*Working with people of difference*

Work is the first step in accepting a person outside of their race, religion, and ethnic culture. This is a fairly easy thing to do. Mainly because we know it is a basic requirement of keeping our jobs. It's hard to imagine an employee telling his manager that "I'm uncomfortable working with the women that are in this department." We know the response will be, "If you are, get comfortable quickly or find another job." Of course, if normal work conditions apply, within two to three years, the differences and feelings of discomfort that might have been there in the beginning are not in time, even thought about. The transition comes about when people really get to know each other.

It is the next several levels that might require a little more effort to get comfortable with the differences that people might have. Let's take a look at those next levels that might present a challenge to a person's comfort zones and might cause him to pre-judge a person before getting to know them.

Step or Level Two – *The Education of your children*

After becoming comfortable with the people with whom you work, the next challenge is to become comfortable with whom your children are attending school. This becomes very personal because of the impact you feel it will have on your cultural traditions and values for future generations via your children. Historically, we can remember the emotional reaction to Black students being blocked by George Wallace from entering Little Rock High School or the violent bus burnings that happen in South Boston when people didn't want their children to go to school with Black children.

Step or Level Three – *The neighbors who moved next door*

Once you are comfortable that your children are happy with their schoolmates and even discover that some of their new best friends might be children of different races, religions, and cultures; it is now time to be concerned about your neighborhood and the new neighbors that are of a different culture that bought the house next door. The concern short term might be discomfort but maybe even fear. The longer-term concern may be the worry about the decline of the neighborhood and the drop in the value of your home.

However, if you get to know those new neighbors, it usually doesn't take long before you are talking over the fence and borrowing each other's lawn tools or a cup of milk when stores are closed. As mentioned, this happened to me and my family even in the racially tense times of the forties and fifties.

Step or Level Four – *My Saturday night social circle*

This is a level that can really test your statement that "some of my best friends are (pick a group)." A good test to take is at your next party where you have invited your friends. The test is to simply count how many of those friends are from a different racial, ethnic, or religious group than you. It is so easy to say I am fluent and comfortable with other cultures but as the unwritten rules state, "A picture is worth a thousand words," "Talk is cheap," and "Seeing is believing."

Step or Level Five – *Guess who's coming to dinner.... permanently?*

This is a level where there is no question that your future generations will be affected by exposure to other cultures. It is whom your children will marry. To have them marry outside of your ethnic, racial, or religious group could almost be for some, too much to bear. In the fifties, I can remember many families disowning their children because they married outside their culture. As strange as it may seem today, at that time, many a Protestant family disowned a child because they married a Catholic or a Jew who married a gentile, or a White that married a Black. Not always the case, but often the discomfort of that marriage was often swept away the moment the first grandchild arrived. Once a grandparent holds their new and beautiful grandchild in their arms, prejudiced opinions seem to just fade away.

Step or Level Six – *Religion*

The final test of how comfortable a person might be with other cultures is surrounded by religion. In a majority Christian religious nation, Sunday morning between ten and twelve is still the most segregated time in our nation. This area is so emotional with people that it is the only area of the six where people are willing to kill other people to protect or reinforce their beliefs. It goes back as far back as the Crusades, to the battle between the Catholics and Protestants in Ireland and the current killings that are going on at the hands of Islamic terrorists and white supremes. All were, and in many cases, still willing to kill for their beliefs.

As Americans, we might want to think that it could never happen to us but a few years ago, a man was sentenced to death in Florida for killing a doctor that performed legal abortions. When he was given his sentence he said, "If I had to do it over again, I would. My God and my beliefs told me I had to do it."

All this tells us that the struggle to be comfortable with other cultures, whether it be race, ethnicity, or religion is not going to be resolved simply by working with people who are different than we are. However, my experience has told me that no matter where you place yourself in the levels outlined above, the moment you start to interact with a person and get to know them; the stereotypes you had start to fade. When you meet others of that group who also don't fit into the stereotypes you had, there could be a tendency to stop pre-judging individuals but instead, begin to judge a person by the content of their character and not their differences. That's not to say by accepting that one person, you will automatically like all people from that group, but you might be more open to reserve judgment until you get to know that next individual as the person they are and not as a stereotype. Until we can learn to do that, we can always convince ourselves that "some of my best friends are...., because I work with two of them and we get along just fine."

CHAPTER SEVEN

THE DYNAMICS OF STEREOTYPING OR BEING STEREOTYPED

WHY DO WE DO IT?

Stereotyping is something we all have done and often have been stereotyped by other people. What is it, why do we do it and where do we get our stereotypes? The dictionary defines stereotyping as "conforming to an unvarying pattern or manner, lacking any individuality."

Herein lies a major fallacy. Have you ever or can you imagine any person that does not have individuality? Even cars have individuality. To think that people would fit into and be totally defined by that category is unimaginable. People are more like snowflakes; everyone's a little different.

Stereotyping is simply putting people in categories or boxes without a close examination. This process allows us to evaluate people and their worth before we get to know them. We do this for a variety of reasons, but mainly because it is easy. Taking the time to get to know people takes a lot of time and effort. Other reason to stereotype is that we are looking for social acceptance. We might decide to adopt the hostilities or other attitudes of the group we are trying to please or join. Another reason is if we have low esteem of ourselves, and by labeling another group as our inferiors, we can make ourselves feel better about ourselves. But more than likely, we stereotype because it is a natural way to organize data. It is so much easier to learn the traits and behaviors of any group of people and then observe whether that individual matches the known traits of their group.

Stereotyping can also be done for safety and personal protection. If we know the groups we should avoid, we can ensure that we will not be endangered by members of that group. Stereotyping can also be of help to members of any group as to their expected code of conduct. This makes it easier to assess a person's potential. Whenever a person does not play out their expected stereotypical behavior, they can often expect to hear statements like, "You're different than other people I've met from your group" or "you're a real credit to your race." This can easily be translated by that stereotyped person as, "I still think members of your group are awful people, but somehow you happen to be different from them." "Yeah" for me, but "ouch" for my culture or race.

All of these reasons might sound like stereotyping can be helpful but in reality, it will usually lead us to unfairly judge individuals and could be a major barrier to developing relationships with people of other cultures.

WHERE DO WE GET OUR STEREOTYPES?

The traits of any group are learned as soon as we can absorb information about any group of people. This knowledge of any group's expected traits can come from messages we receive from our parents and other family members, the TV shows and movies we watch, the jokes that we hear, and even the nightly news that we watch. For fifty years I have conducted a stereotyping exercise in my diversity classroom sessions where I put the titles of identifiable groups on separate charts. These groups included Blacks, Asians, Hispanics, Women, Gays and Lesbians, Older workers, and even White Males. I then instructed the participants to walk around and list all the stereotypical traits that (not them) but society have of those groups. In fifty years, the elements on those charts have never changed. It is an indication that we all have been indoctrinated by the same images and in our subconsciousness, all of us know "How those people are." The stereotype traits of all of our cultural groups are baked into our subconsciousness. The interesting thing I discovered about the charts is that all the traits on each chart were negative except for two. Let me show you the typical listing of the charts to see if you would agree with, again, not your personal beliefs but how society views each group. Let's imagine that whatever group with which you can identify is a collar that you must wear around your neck every day.

As an example, let me use the "Black" collar that I have worn all of my life, but the logic applies to all of the collars that exist. Here is the typical listing of the black stereotype chart. See if you would agree with how society (not you personally) views my group.

The Black Stereotypical Chart

DRUG ADDICTS/PUSHERS	Poor
UNEDUCATED	On Welfare
SINGLE PARENTS	Overly Religious
LAZY	Not Career Oriented
LOW MORALS	Clannish
VIOLENT PEOPLE	Play "Victims"
CHIP ON SHOULDER	**Good Music/Food**
DISHONEST	**Great Athletes**

The first thing you might notice with the labels on the Black chart is that they are all negative except for the last two entries. If it only takes displaying one or two traits on your chart before you are considered "typical" by anyone who doesn't fight stereotyping people, you can see how difficult it is for anyone not to fall victim to their chart. Simply by mispronouncing a word could equate to being UNEDUCATED, sitting at the Black lunch table equals CLANNISH BEHAVIOR, or merely talking about race equals PLAYING THE RACE OR "VICTIM" CARD. Over a period of time, it is close to impossible not to display one of the above behaviors. Once that is done, the judging party may simply assume, given time, many of the other traits will follow with the bottom line being NOT CAREER ORIENTED.

Even the two positive traits can have a powerful impact on young people in the Black community. Since every young person wants to be rich and famous and since on the Black chart being a great entertainer or athlete has been a proven door opener to fame and fortune, is it any wonder that a Black child in the inner city doesn't have a basketball in his or her hands by the time they are five or six. We marvel at the number of Black players that are in the NBA but it is the natural path that most inner city youngsters take because of the successful role models that they have available to them. This can also be seen in music. If a rap group can get young people out of their current living environments, why not start a rap group?

The two other logical professions that are available for young Black children to role-model are; to become a minister whom they have always seen as individuals that have leadership roles and carry much respect in their community or to become drug dealers that have much power and financial success on the negative side of their society.

Let's look at some other collars or charts:

The Women's stereotypical Chart

LIKE TO GOSSIP	Poor Drivers
EMOTIONAL	Can't Handle Pressure
MOODY	Can't Handle Feedback
DETAIL ORIENTED	Can't Handle Money
LOVE TO SHOP	Catty
NOT SERIOUS ABOUT CAREER	**Family Oriented**
OVERLY SENSITIVE	**Nurturing/Caring**

As with the Black chart, the Women's chart is mainly negative and has two glaring positives, that being nurturing/caring and family oriented. This, of course, funnels many young girls into the occupations of nursing, teaching, human resources, and administrative careers. Once a woman is considered "typical" by members of management, there is clearly no reason to consider their leadership potential or even mentor them with tough feedback, as they just might break down and cry.

The Asian Stereotypical Chart

GOOD AT MATH	Non-Social
COMPUTER LITERATE	Clannish
HIGHLY EDUCATED	Sly
FOLLOWERS	Devious
SHY AND PASSIVE	**Technically Oriented**
SNEAKY	**Hard Working**

Needless to say that the negatives on the Asian chart clearly tell us that they cannot be senior managers or high-level executives in an organization but that's OK with them. All they want is to stay to themselves and work hard on their technical careers.

The Hispanic Stereotypical Chart

The list of negatives includes such things as they don't fit in nor want to, are lazy, not career-oriented, and have an immigrant mentality. But on the positive side, they have good music and good food. Bottom-line, they wouldn't make good management candidates.

The Gay, Lesbian, and Transgender Chart

Their list of negatives includes such things as immoral, angry, and clannish, but they are creative and artistic but not a good fit for business or management.

Older Worker Stereotypical Chart

Negatives include being slow, mentally checked out, not open to new ideas, just waiting for retirement, and technically deficient but they do have great "War stories" about the days gone by. Organizations should give them a "golden parachute" retirement offer and get them out of the way.

The Younger Worker Stereotypical Chart

They of course think they know it all, don't respect traditions, are not serious about work or career but can be paid less until they grow up.

We have listed just a few of the collars that exist in our society. There are so many more. They include such trivial things as being tall, short, fat, what part of the country you were raised in, what school you attended, your socio-economic status and so many more. The bottom line to all of them is their charts are all basically negative with no group having the option of being identified with a positive group except one. That is, having the collar of a White male. It is the only group in our nation that has a positive set of traits on its chart. Let's take a look at that chart.

The White Male Stereotypical Chart

DEPENDABLE	Leaders
RESPONSIBLE	Powerful
INFLUENTIAL	Trustworthy
PILLARS OF COMMUNITY	Strategic Thinkers
FAMILY ORIENTED	Savvy
DECISION MAKERS	**Insensitive of Other Groups**
COMPETITIVE	**Feel Superior to Others**

Immediately, we can see a blaring difference in the perception of the White Male chart versus all of the others. All of their traits are positive and only two are negative. It is exactly the flip flop of every other's group chart. With these positive stereotypes, there can be no doubt as to what group an organization would go to for the selection of their managers and executives. As to the two negatives concerning their insensitivity and feeling of superiority, all it takes is a four-hour awareness/sensitivity training session and that is enough to fix those issues.

Of course, that was a touch of sarcasm. Just as you can't become fluent in French with one French lesson, nor can you change the way of thinking of a lifetime in a four-hour diversity session. So, many members of this group can comfortably say that, "If it ain't really broke, why should we fix it." In essence, the thought is, "We as White males have successfully handled the leadership roles since this country began, there is no reason to change." This has been a winning strategy for White males in the past, but with the changes that are going on in this country and on the current world stage, it might be time for White males to review their strategies moving forward.

Let's first look at the changes that are happening in our organizations. As the workforce has changed and is predicted to continue changing, the White male chart will change as well. The collars worn by White males will in the future, be viewed by Women, People of Color, and immigrants (who will make up seventy percent of the workforce) through a different set of lenses. If we now look at the White male chart through the eyes of today's changing workforce, the chart looks more like this.

White Male Stereotypical Chart as seen by Women and Minorities

CONCEITED	Insensitive
DOMINEERING	Chauvinistic
CAN'T BE TRUSTED	Closed Network
"MY WAY OR THE HIGHWAY"	Racist
AMBITIOUS	Play Favorites
BROWN NOSES	Feel Superior
NO PRINCIPLES	Elitist
PREJUDICED	Hypocritical

As we can see, through the eyes of the changing workforce, White Males no longer have a free pass as to the only positive chart. Their collar now becomes one of the most negative as viewed by our current changing workforce. The impact on them is two-fold. One is trying to handle the growing lack of trust that now might exist between them and the changing demographics of their team. It was bad enough when the one or two women or minorities that were in his charge mistrusted him, but now when the majority of his team has that mistrust or won't support him fully with his mission, success for the White male becomes much more difficult.

The other negative factor, like all collars, forces him to walk on eggshells, having to watch everything he does or says to prevent displaying any one of the new negative traits that they now carry on their new chart. Using the same rule that all you have to do is display one negative trait and it could then be assumed that you would display the other traits if given enough time; you can see the potential negative assumptions that a diverse staff could have about their White manager when that manager makes merely one insensitive comment at a staff meeting. White males must now spend much of their thought processes making sure they do not do or say things that might be viewed as "politically incorrect" if they want to maintain the trust and loyalty of their staff members.

This is a major reason why so many white males hate that they must always be "politically correct" and that they now carry the label of being "The angry white male." That is the impact of being stereotyped. He must now, like all other groups, become aware of his collar and spend a lot of effort making sure that he does not display any element on his chart. This, of course, is a major distraction for everyone and keeps people from concentrating on getting their jobs done. It just makes everyone angry when you are forced to do it.

KNOWING YOUR OWN STEREOTYPES

As we have seen, we all know every other group's stereotypes but everyone must become a Ph.D. on their own group's traits. Remember, one of the major reasons we all utilize the stereotyping process is because of the time it saves. To truly get to know an individual requires time with that person. This knowledge comes from the conversations you have with them and the observations you make of the behaviors and attitudes they display on a variety of subjects. In time, you can collect enough data to come up with fairly accurate conclusions about that individual.

But who has all of that time to spare? Not many of us do. A much faster method is to merely identify the collar of the group to which that person belongs and then just observe if they display any of the traits of their group. If that person does display some of the traits (a minimum of one might be enough, two cements it), you can quickly come to the conclusion that if you had more time with that individual, you would probably see many of the other traits for which their group is known. The expression of confirmation usually comes with the statement, "He's or she's a typical (fill in the blank). On a multi-cultural work team, that one racial or ethnic joke at a staff meeting or at a team gathering at a bar by a White manager could leave that manager totally ineffective with his team. It is now safe to say that the wearing of stereotypical collars has crippled every group of our workforce, even White males. Of course, in many cases that quick evaluation may be miles away from an accurate assessment, but who cares. It was at least done without a large expenditure of your time.

Knowing now that it only takes displaying one or two traits that are on your chart before many will conclude that you are a typical representative of your group, then it is essential that a person learns all of their group's traits if they don't want important decision makers to draw a negative conclusion about them before they have had a chance to get to know who they really are. This can be seen in the scenario of a woman making sure that she doesn't openly show emotion in a business discussion or in my case forty years ago to make sure I didn't pick up a piece of watermelon in the company cafeteria or order the fried chicken at lunch.

Back in the seventies and eighties, it was a standard joke among Black employees who came together for a quick discussion that "We've been together too long, we better break up before everyone starts to think that we are planning a revolution." It has been proven by many experiments that when people have to concentrate so much on their collars just to survive, they become less productive.

In today's world, it would not be "politically correct" to say out loud that someone is "a typical ......   " but all of this process operates at our subconscious level. This simply means that we make decisions about people without knowing how we came to our conclusions. We often just tell ourselves, "I just got a good or bad feeling about that guy." No facts, just "my gut feel" and we are always told to trust our gut. That may be good advice if we have updated the messages in our gut-level tape recorders on which those decisions are being made but could lead to some very bad decisions if we have not.

It is so easy to tell yourself that since I don't display the traits on my chart, I'm just not going to worry about it. Unfortunately, you don't have the power to make those decisions about yourself. Other people will be the judge of you, and they just might not have the skills of knowing how to avoid stereotyping people that you might have. Unfortunately, as an individual, the only power you have in other people's perception of you is to ensure you do not act in a stereotypical manner with the people you are around. Sometimes, this is enough to keep you off of your group's negative chart and sometimes it is not. There are some who might not have to observe any traits, they just assume when they see a collar, that person is what they imagine him or her to be from the very instant they first walk into the room. Gender and skin color can drive some people to an instant evaluation of that person.

If you think you have it bad because you own one of the negative labels or collars we have listed above, imagine how it is for individuals that own multiple collars. For example, what if you were an older, disabled, Hispanic, lesbian, Muslim woman and had to fight all of those charts every time you stepped out of the house. For me, it is hard to picture them even wanting to get out of bed every morning. For those with multiple collars, even if they do bravely take on the world, it is hard to imagine what little time they would have doing creative, productive work always having to think about the do's and do not's of each one of their many labels. When you know that one displayed negative trait from any one of the five groups by which they can be identified might sidetrack their career, it can turn into a full-time job all by itself. My two collars of an older African-American are more than enough to keep me busy.

YOU STILL CAN BE IN CONTROL

All of these so far are defensive action steps and should be considered. However, a way to gain greater control of the perception people may have of you is to go on the offense. This means becoming an astute and effective game player. The better you become at playing effectively by the rules of the mainstream game, the quicker people will forget about putting you on any chart other than the "game player" chart. A nice chart to be on if you want to reach your career objectives.

If the positive traits on the white male chart are the elements from which promotions are made, it might be logical to start displaying those traits in yourself. If you review those positive traits that are on the white male chart, you will notice they are the traits that are connected to leadership. None of them are exclusive to skin color, gender, sexual orientation, or any other chart. It may, however, require you to go through personal change, breaking out of your comfort zones and maybe even adjusting some of your current relationships. In reality, you still have total control of your image and actions. That means doing things that could enhance your status and not display traits of your culture that could be labeled as typical.

Remember, the changes that you might be considering are not changes that are making you "White" but are ones that are taking you closer to the American mainstream and to higher positions in your organization. Mainstream America has a little of all of our cultures within it so no one needs to feel that they are selling out.

BUT WHY CAN'T I JUST BE ME?

This gets us into the discussions of "It's not fair that I can't just be me" or "Why can't the system respect my culture?" Or "If I do the things that the system demands, it doesn't allow me to be me." I think the current expression with young people today is "Don't I have the right to be my 'authentic self.'" All of these questions are valid ones to consider, but the bottom line is fairly simple. How badly do you want to accomplish or reach the career goals you have set for yourself? I know in my life; I have changed my "authentic self" many times over. Every major life change I have made has forced me to look at my authentic self and often has forced me to change that definition to be successful in the new roles I have taken on. Some that instantly jumped out to me are the transition I made from single to married and having my first child. Our system does not care what cultural community anyone decides in which they want to live or the roles they want to take on in their lives. Our system leaves those choices up to us as individuals and since 1964 and the passage of the Civil Rights Act, from a business perspective, we are now all free to choose what we want our authentic selves to be. I have found that it does not take long when we redefine our authentic self that we soon become comfortable in that new definition. Often, we grow to like the new definition better than the old one that was replaced.

If your parents were like mine, you probably heard from them growing up that "No one ever said that life was going to be fair." That statement might apply to almost everyone that is playing this game of life, with the exception of some white men that grew up as WASPs, (White Anglo-Saxon Protestant males). Remember the rule, "Whoever is at the top of a pyramid has the right to make the rules." That would mean that this game is not "fair" for most women, people of color, people living at lower socioeconomic levels, immigrants, people of any religion, (with the exception of Protestant), people of a different sexual orientation, the disabled and the list goes on and on. As you might imagine, it would be impossible to have a set of rules or a culture in which everyone would start from the same starting block and be immediately comfortable with the system. This is the sole reason we have a mainstream culture.

The mainstream culture is the language where any individual of any culture can change their behaviors in order to be able to reach their life's goals. Is it easier for members of the WASP reservation to adopt? Absolutely, for that culture has had a major impact on mainstream rules being one of the first cultures to define what the rules are. So, to have been born into and have grown up in that culture means it is their native language. But as more cultures come into the mainstream, it is requiring those WASPs to make personal adjustments as well and at a minimum, are being forced to compete with an expanding number of qualified people from many different cultures.

Making the change to mainstream rules

Is making the change to mainstream America a difficult thing to do? Not so much from a practical perspective. The behaviors and activities of mainstream America are not really difficult to learn. Most of the activities can comfortably be mastered in one or two years. It's like the fluency process we discussed earlier. It might be a little more difficult to change accents, word pronunciations, and if an immigrant, even having to learn a new language. The real difficulty is making the mental decision that you want to change and evaluating if the effort is worth the reward.

In the world of fiction, Liza Doolittle did it in the musical My Fair Lady by changing herself from a lower class flower girl to an upper class women. In a real-life situation, Margaret Thatcher had to make major changes in her life to accomplish the goals she had set for herself. This included having to take speech lessons to get rid of a squeaky-sounding voice she felt diminished her image of being a strong leader. In both examples, a lot of work was involved, but also in both cases they felt that the changes they had to make were well worth the aggravation they had to go through to address what was needed to reach their career or life objectives. Will Rogers, the once great philosopher and entertainer, once said in this life that is forever changing, "When you're through changing, then you are through."

One of the negative aspects of the positive stereotype chart for a White male is they are expected to be a leader, even if they don't want to be. As a result, they end up being a disappointment to many people who looked for greater things from that White individual. It's sort of the old "Whites man burden" to make sure that things are run properly. To have to bear the expectations of others to do something that you do not want to do, is an awful burden to carry. However, for the White male that wants to be a leader, they have a true advantage over everyone else that is not on the White chart. Being successful and a leader is just expected of them.

This does not mean that women and/or people of color cannot compete. But it might be logical to assume that people not raised in a mainstream environment might have a more difficult job in making the transition. However, if anyone ever starts to feel sorry for themselves, I ask you to just think about the advantage you might have over a transgender person or a person that has to spend their entire life in a wheelchair. The key is to accept who you are, understand the hurdles you might be confronted with, set the objectives you want to accomplish in your life, and as Nike would say, "Just Do It!"

Remember what we said about the older, disabled, gay, Muslim, and Hispanic women. She would be wearing six collars that all would be considered negative by our society. No matter how bad we might think our situation might be, there is usually someone that is worse off. It is also entirely possible that an African-American woman raised in a country club environment and whose parents are doctors, lawyers, or successful corporate executives; and a white male with a similar background, might have an equal or level playing field. On the other hand, a White male coming from a coal mining family will not have the same starting point on their road to success. White skin and the male gender are not guarantees for success in this game we are playing but those who choose to venture into the mainstream, knowing how our system works can be a great equalizer for all.

PROBLEM-SOLVING TECHNIQUES TO AVOID STEREOTYPING

We have established that we learn the stereotypical traits of groups as early as we are able to input information. We mentioned that they come in the form of ethnic, racial, and gender jokes, the TV shows and movies we watch, from our personal observations, and even from the 6:00 news broadcast. I have often stated that someone new to our country could watch the news for one month and could duplicate every chart that we listed earlier. On any given broadcast, we can see an African-American story that covers a violent crime, a drug store, stories that cover lower socio-economic and/or working-class Blacks, and then will switch to stories that show Blacks in a sports or entertainment role. After a month of repetition of these stories, it would be easy to conclude. "It's obvious, that's how those people are." Not shown in the news will be stories of the African-Americans going about the normal American activities of doing their jobs at work and functioning as good neighbors in the typical integrated suburban neighborhood. But why should the news broadcast those stories? That kind of news just doesn't sell.

Let's then review a list of items that one might consider that will help avoid pre-judging people through the stereotyping method:

- One must make a special conscious effort not to put anyone in a box when they first meet them.
- Take the time to get to know people as individuals and not see them as a member of a group.
- Expand your social circle beyond your current cultural group
- Try to learn more about the cultures of people you meet

- **Try Judging everyone with a blank sheet of paper**

This is a point that might deserve some additional attention. What it suggests is, if you can rid yourself of the many negative traits that we have been taught about all groups of people, we may then be able to greet everyone we meet with a blank sheet of paper. If this can be done, then we can put on that person's chart only the things that we can personally observe coming from that individual. This is the only way we can accurately access the true nature and character of any individual. Even when they display what you might consider is a negative trait, you very well might have observed seven or eight positive traits that will more than outweigh that one negative trait.

That one negative trait then simply becomes a self-improvement objective that you can consider sharing with that person to help them with their development or if in a social environment, it might be that one negative quirk that most of our best friends have. We just tolerate it. That negative trait becomes nothing more than "that's just the way Fred is, but he really is a good guy." After all, who of us can say that we are perfect?

CHAPTER EIGHT

BRIDGING CULTURAL TRUST GAPS

Having individuals and teams being able to communicate effectively with each other is, of course, essential for relationships to grow and for strong team cooperation to be achieved. A major barrier to this happening is the "Trust Gaps" that exist between individuals, departments, organizations, and even nations. There are very few things that can destroy effective communication connections more than mistrust. When you mistrust someone, it is difficult to take anything said as being sincere or trustworthy. If this occurs, it can have a domino effect of not hearing what an individual is really saying and/or reacting negatively to messages that have been falsely received, thus straining personal relationships and even leading to less effective teams.

Trust gaps are created by our stereotypes, prejudices, past life experiences, our value systems, and our gut feelings, just to name a few. They can occur between any two people that differ in race, ethnic background, gender, age, socio-economic levels, regions of the country, political philosophies, neighborhoods, religion, levels of power, work departments, disciplines, sexual orientation, physical appearance, and please stop me, this could go on for a long time. I think we can get the picture. As people, we are all different and any of our differences can create a trust gap between any two people with whom we work and/or socialize. Since the game is about people, it is critical that we recognize trust gaps when they occur and take steps to eliminate them whenever possible.

COMMUNICATING ACROSS CULTURAL AND GENDER GAPS

Communicating across race, gender, ethnicity, age, and sexual orientation gaps are of particular concern in organizations as the workforce continues to become more diverse. When these gaps are not addressed by individuals and leadership in an organization, history has shown us that those gaps will continually grow wider, and the consequences can be severe. Organizations can expect higher turnover, more employee negative situations that must be resolved by HR, and a decrease in employee cooperation and morale. All affect the mission or bottom line of that organization. For individuals, the effect can be teammates avoiding one another, strained relationships between managers and employees, and can create an environment that just is no fun in which to work.

GOOD INTENTIONS CAN BECOME NEGATIVE MESSAGES

Have you ever said something to a person that you thought was a positive comment and later found out that you had insulted that individual? If you have, you would have experienced the power of a trust gap. It has the ability to totally change any message from positive to negative. The significance of this is, of course, understanding that our messages are not the ones that we send; they are the messages that the ones hearing them, take away. Our intended message is only useful to ourselves but does nothing positive for the receiver if they do not hear our positive intent. One can easily brush this off with a comment like, "Well, if they are so sensitive or have hang-ups, that's their concern, not mine." That could be true, but if the negative message is received by your boss or from one of your direct reports whose support and the best effort are needed by you, then it can very much become your concern as well.

An example of how the trust gap can change a message between genders can be as simple as how questions can be perceived. Let's look at a scenario when a new male employee is invited out for a drink by his male manager after work on the first day. The intent would be to get to know that employee a little better and to answer any questions they may have after their first day on the job. A noble mission for any manager to undertake. Over that drink, the manager asks his employee if he is married, what does his wife do for a living, how many kids does he have, and whether are they all settled in school. After that exchange, it is difficult for any man to walk away not thinking what a great boss he has. He obviously cares about me, my family, and my welfare.

Let's take a look at that same scenario and what might happen if that new employee was a woman and there exists a gender trust gap. The invitation to go out for a drink after the first day of work might immediately produce a red flag. Her major concern might be wondering if he invites all new employees to have a drink on their first day, or am I an exception? It might be a custom for that manager to do so, but if that is not disclosed, the invitation will be accepted but possibly under a cloud of suspicion.

At the table, without thinking about it, the same questions will be asked but the trust gap may take over and translate them into an entirely different meaning. For example, the question "Are you married?" Translation: "Is he hitting on me." The question of "What does your husband do?" Translation: Why does he need to know that? If I tell him he is a Vice President, will he conclude I don't really need this job, and will it affect future promotions and raises?" The question of "How many kids do you have?" Translation: "I have to tell him four children and will he think that I am not career oriented and can be relied on for long hours and travel?"

You can see it is the same scenario. The same positive intent was meant with both conversations but it is possible that it established a very shaky beginning for the male/female work relationship. It is no one's fault that this happens; it just happens. Of course, it is very possible that it will not happen at all. That will all depend on the life experiences of both parties, the way the messages are delivered, and the sensitivity of the boss to read the non-verbal of that new employee. If the employee is uncomfortable and the manager is observant, he should be able to pick up on the messages of that employee and ensure she understands the reasons for his questions. Also understanding, by "walking in another person's shoes" the manager might consider changing locations for that first "get acquainted" session. It might be better to have lunch in the company cafeteria than in a local bar.

"But I am often told that one should treat everyone the same. After all, you don't want people to think you have favorites." That is true. If you are a manager, being consistent in the treatment of all employees is very important. Team members can quickly spot when a manager is showing preferential treatment to any one or two individuals. This, of course, causes mistrust to grow even more. However, consistently treating everyone fairly does not always mean treating everyone the same.

A good example of this is a parent of three children. You learn very quickly that if you treat all three children the same, you might lose effectiveness with two of them. And so, we as parents learn very quickly how each child must be handled to best get important messages through to them. Why and how do we do this? We want the best for all three children so we take the time to study each one of them and learn about their individual needs. We then can make the necessary adjustments to be effective with each child. That caring and taking time to get to know members of our family is the same formula that can prove to be successful at work.

"HE/SHE DIDN'T MEAN ANYTHING BY THAT"

This is the comment that is normally made by a person who has closed the trust gap with an individual and is trying to explain to another member of their group that the person in question can be trusted. As an example, what happens when a white person I know very well, walks up to me when I'm with some black friends and says something to me that is normal and comfortable between the two of us but I know his remarks make my black friends uncomfortable? When he walks away, the "He didn't mean anything by that" might be an appropriate comment for me to make to my Black friends. The trust gap may have been closed between me and my white friend but not between them.

Common missteps in sending positively intended messages to people are an indication that the receiver of your message might have some mistrust of you. If so, you will want to quickly dispel their feelings of mistrust. And so in an effort to bridge that gap of mistrust, there could be a tendency to force that gap closer by showing that you are familiar or comfortable with the receiver's culture. This might come in the form of racial, gender, or ethnic jokes (kiss of death), using cultural slang and or hand greetings to show your acceptance of their culture, giving someone a cultural nickname, always bringing up cultural topics, and by stating the old faithful, "Some of my best friends are...   ." All might be well intended, but rarely will they be received in a positive way if the trust gap has not been closed between two people. In many cases, these efforts often drive the trust gap further apart.

CLOSING THE GAP

If so many of these gaps exist with the many people we know and with whom we interact, how can we possibly keep up with where we stand with them all? The best advice that I can give to that very valid question, is to have patience. Don't force relationships. Good relations that are trustworthy will happen in their own good time. The trust gaps that exist between all of us begin to close when we show respect for each other, when we start to listen to each other, when we share information about ourselves and our family and then care enough to ask about theirs. It closes when we feel that we "have each other's backs" and know that when the chips are down, we can count on each other's support. The more we know about each other and discover our similarities, the more we forget about our differences, and the trust gaps start to disappear.

The gap also starts to close when we become sensitive to the mindset of others and to their cultural values. This, however, must be done with people seeing them as individuals and not as a member of a group. Because as we all know, Blacks, Whites, Jews, Gays, Muslims, Women, Transgenders, and Italians do not think alike. Just like our children, we must see everyone as the person they are not the group to which they belong. Is this work? Yes! Is it worth the effort? If the game is about people, and more people with diverse backgrounds will, in the future, be involved in our lives, (both work or social); then that answer is a resounding "Yes, it is worth it!" To make it happen, we must come off our mental, cultural reservations and truly try to see situations through the lenses of the other person's life experiences.

CHAPTER NINE

RACISM/SEXISM IN AMERICA

It was not my intent to make any major comments on racism in this book because so many other books have been written on this important subject. Having lived with it for my entire life, I think I could add to that conversation but I did not want it to be the major theme of this book.

However, after witnessing all the events of 2020/21/22 that involved race, it would be naive of me to ignore it in the journey of America becoming a melting pot of and for all Americans.

RACISM

Yes, we are a racist country. We have always been so and only time will tell if that is our fate forever. How many times, for those who are older, have we thought that we were close to getting beyond racism but were shocked back into reality? For me, I thought it so after our nation's reaction to the murder of Emmett Till in 1954. Clearly, after that horrible incident and the outward showing of remorse that prevail in this country at the time, I was sure things would get better.

After the passage of the Civil Rights and Voting Rights Acts, we all knew that America had put aside race as criterion for success in our country. We did not. Then came the assassination of Dr. King, and the riots of the sixties, seventies, and eighties all telling us that racism still existed but we recommitted to doing better. Since no major incidents had happened for thirty years, we thought racism was no longer a major issue in America and we could move on.

Then came 2020 when all Hell broke loose. The killing of Black citizens by police caught on camera, the formation of Black Lives Matter, and the demonstration of White Supremacists in Charlottesville, Va., all reminded me that racial prejudice is still a major factor in defining who we are as a country. The most we can say after any of the above incidents is "At least we are getting better, it's not as bad as it was in the fifties and sixties."

That is a true statement. We are getting better, but are we getting better fast enough to be able to compete with China, India, and Europe, five generations from now? Can we keep our world leadership position intact with all of our internal racial fighting and by not totally developing and utilizing all of our talent? Clearly, that answer is a resounding "No." As an example, let's just look at one area of future importance; the educational strategies of the United States versus China.

Today, we have twenty million students enrolled in higher education institutions with an average cost of $8,000 per student. Compare that to China which has a higher education student enrollment of forty-five million with an average cost per student of $3,000. At this rate, how long will it take China and its volume of graduating scientists, engineers, computer programmers, doctors, lawyers and so many other fields of studies, until they start to dominate and take over the leadership role of the world? If we do not address the racial inequality in education and address the quality of life issues for all of our citizens, our place as the world leader will be short-lived. Remember, white males by 2060 will only be 29% of the American workforce. We can no longer give quality education opportunities based on race or socio-economic factors. We are going to need all of our children prepared for the future competitive global economy.

SEXISM

Addressing sexism is an equally important issue that we must take on with our full commitment. Giving equal treatment to women should not even be up for discussion. From a moral, ethical point of view, it's just the right thing to do. From a practical point of view, it is insane to believe that we can subjugate fifty-one percent of our population and expect to remain competitive. By 2060, that percentage will increase to be 55% of the people we must rely on to get the job done for us. I am told that nations like Japan and China have fifty-year strategic plans in place to ensure their role in the world's future. I think because of racism and sexism in this country, we have abandoned any long-term visions of what will keep America a leading global power. What we see is our current power structure concentrating on and struggling to maintain its current power base. I'm afraid other nations may be laughing at our short-sightedness.

THE EFFECTS OF SEPARATE BUT EQUAL

From a legal perspective, the issue of "separate but equal" has been decided. The Supreme Court's ruling in Brown v. The Board of Education of Topeka Kansas reversed the ruling in Plessy v. Ferguson stating that separation of races, even if educational facilities are the same, does not make things equal. Some of my life experiences seem to confirm the Supreme Court's decision.

From a race perspective, I grew up in a town in the forties that had a "colored" YMCA and a white one. Our facility consisted of a pool and ping/pong table and a basketball hoop outside. The white Y on the other hand had an indoor basketball court, racket ball courts, an indoor swimming pool, and a locker room. The separation was there but it could in no way be considered equal.

THE IMPACT OF "SEPARATE BUT EQUAL" WITH WOMEN

Many might conclude that this practice has no bearing on gender. After all, the only separation of the genders is with public bathroom and that separation is obvious and practical. However, when we examine gender separation, we might come up with some different conclusions. If there is a dominant culture that separates itself from what our society considers a lesser culture, it can have a powerful impact on both groups. This has clearly been the case with men and women in our country.

My first experience in seeing this firsthand was when I was chairman of the board of the Atlanta Girl's Club. We were separated from the Boy's Club and I had flashbacks to my youth and the separated YMCA's of my childhood. The Boy's Club had a board consisting of very influential business leaders and thus had facilities and financial resources that far exceed those of the Girl's Club. I was dedicated to get the two clubs to join forces. An additional motivation was reading a study that tried to explain why little girls that were competitive with boys in math and science lost that willingness to compete when they reached the age of thirteen.

One conclusion was that this phenomenon happened at the age little boys and girls started to notice that the other gender existed. Because girls at that age have been ingrained by our society to understand that the male culture is dominant and they started to feel, if they wanted to please the boys, they should stop competing with them and just accept their second-class status. Plus, it made them more popular with the boys not to beat them in any competition, which included grades. The women's culture has come a long way since those times but the dominant male culture still has its negative effect on many women today.

In the seminars that I have been conducting just for women for forty years, just twenty years ago, many discussions were held as to how to break the news to their husbands that their last raise made them the leading breadwinner in the family. It was news that they dreaded telling their husbands for fear of their husband's negative reactions. A clear sign that many women still feel that they cannot compete with and exceed the accomplishments of their male partners.

Of course, this is a tremendous hurdle that causes some women to not be all that they can and should be. It, however, has a negative impact on the male culture as well, for it gives many men the belief that women truly are an inferior culture that can't compete with men. Many men are finally starting to realize that they better wake up to modern reality as they see women of today, not only competing but becoming their bosses. The feeling of not being able to stand toe to toe with men is fading quickly with every generation but unfortunately, it still exists with many women even today.

As for the outcome of trying to combine the Boy's and Girl's Club, I am happy to say it did happen on my watch. The organization is now the Boy's and Girl's Club of Atlanta. Maybe one day it might actually become the Girl's and Boy's Club of Atlanta. I won't hold my breath on that but at least the facilities and financial resources are the same for both genders.

SEXUAL ORIENTATION

People with different sexual orientations and those that are transgender are the last of our American brothers and sisters to be reluctantly accepted by the American mainstream. I say reluctantly because of the core basic freedoms for which they are still fighting. Even though we have granted them such basic freedoms such as the right to marry, we still are slow to accept them as equals in our workplaces and our communities.

As a society, we might have done so under our laws but we have not done so, in many environments, with our minds and our hearts. Let's get logical and practical again. Almost five percent of our population is LGBTQ+ and around eighty-eight percent of them are in our workforce. We really don't know the exact percentage because it is estimated that over forty-six percent of LGBTQ+ workers are closeted. It is hard to believe that so many Americans still feel they have to hide who they are to be treated fairly in their job. This community is still waiting for our lawmakers to pass legislation that would give LGBTQ+ workers complete protection from job discrimination in our workplaces. Only twenty states and Washington D.C. have enacted such laws.

Isn't it logical that we should open our workplaces and our minds to the talents and skills that members of the LGBTQ+ community can and have brought to the table? The list of famous American contributors who were LGBTQ+ is far too numerous to name. Even if we did, we would not get a complete list because before the early 1930's it was suicidal to declare to be a person of a different sexual orientation.

There is one American, however, I would like to mention, simply because I think she is one of the most impactful Americans in our history. That person is Eleanor Roosevelt. The work she did for our citizens during our Great Depression and our soldiers during World War II is almost unbelievable. The efforts she made to move race acceptance forward in this country are historic and as a delegate to the United Nations and the writer of its first Declaration on Human Rights, has left a lasting impact on the world. Clearly, we do not want to overlook that kind of talent in our current and future workforce simply because we can't learn to accept people just for the content of their character.

THE DISABLED

Attention to this community is and should be ongoing. Fortunately, we realized the wasted potential of our disabled community and passed "The Americans with Disabilities Act" so that they can make their valuable contributions to our society and improve their quality of life. Things like revamping buildings, providing signing at conferences, and tools to help disabled workers overcome their disadvantages have gone a long way to make them become more productive citizens. We must continually look for ways to bring more disabled workers comfortably into our workforce. If we do, we might find another Franklin Roosevelt who brought us out of the Great Depression and saved the world from Fascism. The discrimination of many groups in the workplace is still a major problem that has to be expelled before we can tap into the total talents of our disabled population as well as develop environments that will allow all American workers to reach their full potential.

THE SOLUTION TO PREJUDICE

The best solution to the problem of prejudice in our great country is simple, we should just stop pre-judging people. It sounds so simple but as a nation, we just can't seem to put our national arms around these many centuries-old dilemmas. One of the major reasons for this happening is, we just don't know each other. Too many of us spend our entire lives on our reservations and miss out on the richness of diversity that we, as individuals, can experience. I know we like to visit other cultures on vacations and enjoy those experiences but they are temporary experiences that allow us to come home to our comfortable cultural reservations.

The fact is, the vast majority of Americans have friends or family members who are gay, lesbian, transgender, or disabled, and we love them. This is possible because we have come to know them as smart, creative, caring, and beautiful people. We accept them just the way they are. We can have that kind of connection with anyone if we take the time to go below that first layer of skin color, gender, and sexual orientation. To not do so will force us to go into our "gut level tape recorders" and draw on the stereotype characteristics that we have described in the last chapter.

When we leave our gut and start thinking with our brains, I think we will do the right thing. As for the LGBT community, as an example, we will honestly ask ourselves, "Why should some of our fellow citizens in the professed, freest nation in the world, have to feel they must hide their "authentic" self in a closet to be successful. America should be a room where there are no closets to have to come out of. If we could just walk that mile in another person's shoes, I can't imagine anyone wanting to live in that kind of situation. Having the freedom to be able to be themselves openly and proudly because our society will accept them for the content of their character, is an America in which we all could be proud.

Just one more suggestion for a solution. This is a situation that will not be corrected by laws and organizational policy statements. If prejudice is to be eradicated, it will be up to each individual American to make it happen. One of the biggest mistakes that organizational America has made is abandoning awareness and sensitivity training. I have taught these courses since 1967 and they clearly made a difference in the attitudes of managers and employees at a time that America could not have been more divided on racial and gender issues. For the past two generations, awareness and sensitivity training has been reduced, in most organizations to an hour on-line seminar on sub-conscious prejudice. That just is not good enough when the eruption that racism has shown itself to be so prevalent in our society today.

I often hear that we should not be concerned in that the older generation will soon retire or die off and those old attitudes will fade from the workforce. I fear that will not be the case. Although many of our young people have grown up with greater contact with people who are different from themselves more so than was the case fifty years ago, many still have grown up with various mental and cultural reservations and need some help in working through the challenges of living in a diverse society.

As a nation, the most important long term solution is the need to focus on educating our children. Not just the children of the wealthy and middle class, but all American children. We became a world power partly due to us realizing the importance of providing free public education to all American children in early 1900. Later we extended via the Land Grant legislation, inexpensive college education, mainly in the areas of agriculture and engineering, to our young people. We had the foresight to realize that our future power lay in the education of our children. In contrast, our children today must go into life-long debt in order to get a college education. As a result, many of our lower socio-economic children have given up hope of ever going to college. The expense of college today is furthering the gap between the haves and have-nots and is leaving behind many of the children we will need if we are to remain a world power.

We need to help our young people continue with their education beyond high school, whether it be four-year degrees or vocational schools as we did with high school education in the past. It made a tremendous difference then and can do so again. Maybe we will reinvest in this critical area again if we understand its importance to the future success of our organizations and our nation. Our workforce is going to become much more diverse than it is today and we need to give our workers the tools to deal with the changes they will experience. By providing affordable education for all, we can turn our future children from being a burden on our society to becoming productive citizens and contributors to our future greatness.

A final suggestion for us as individuals is to start forging a successful future by reducing the growing prejudice we are displaying toward each other. This will require us to come off our mental reservations, at least long enough to get to know each other. When and if we do, we will find that a lot of people in our many cultures have the same values and life objectives as we do. We, as Americans, have a lot in common.

CHAPTER TEN

SHARING YOUR JOURNEY WITH OTHERS

There are some who travel the journey we are all on in this life alone. But most people at some point and time, share their journey with other people. These people might include family, friends, husbands, wives, and partners. If you meet and connect with a mate at the same socio- economic level, more than likely the two of you will have many things in common as it relates to interests, hobbies, and life activities. You might also have similar outlooks on values, life perspectives and basically what you feel is important as it relates to such issues as, how to raise children and even what you consider are the fun things to do.

All of this can change, and often does when one of the partners decides to move their careers to the next higher socio-economic level. When that happens, the partner who wants to advance will more than likely start to learn new activities and thus become involved with a new circle of people connected to those new activities. It could be as simple as quitting the bowling team and joining a bridge club or tennis team. At the lower levels of the game board, (which consists of seven levels), such as level three or level four, it is entirely possible for both members of that relationship to go their separate ways with their activities without major consequences. The only requirement might be to go to the final bowling or tennis banquet with your partner, and then settle back into the routine of your own regular lifestyle activities.

This can happen very easily and without much disruption in the relationship until you reach the fifth level of the game. If you hold a job at level three or four, you can usually work that job and then go home to the social life in which you are comfortable. There are rarely social obligations connected to work. This is often not the case once you are promoted to a position that exists at level five. It is at this level that often your job requires you to entertain customers or clients at restaurants, represent your organization at the Chamber of Commerce or the Urban League annual dinner when your organization has purchased a table, and expect you and your significant other to be there to represent them. As you move even higher on the organizational ladder, you might even be expected, at a minimum to attend your boss's annual Christmas party or even be expected to hold a party at your home. In doing so, it allows all of your potential future sponsors to see if you have developed a partnership that has grown comfortable interacting at that higher level and the two of you can be seen as a team that they may recommend for even higher positions. This is a way they can match people with the future social requirements that those higher positions will demand.

LET'S TALK TENNIS

The dynamics with those scenarios described above are two-fold. The one partner that has begun to learn the lifestyle of that upper level will become comfortable with the activities and conversations at any social gathering because they have experienced those activities and have learned what is required to fit in at the table. The partner that has not bothered to learn the activities and lifestyle that are being discussed (let's take tennis as an example) will feel out of place and might divert the conversation to a discussion about their interest which might happen to be bowling this is at first interesting to the table but that interest fades very quickly. No one feels less of the bowler because most at the table, at one time were in a bowling league themselves and very much enjoyed that experience. But "that was then and this is now." There is no problem with the acceptance of that partner at the table. Everyone will assess that he or she is a very nice person. The problem becomes when a future potential sponsor has to assess if the two individuals, as a team, have prepared yourselves to be effective at a higher socio-economic level that the higher positions will require.

THAT'S NOT FAIR

A person's first thought might be, "That's not fair! I can do my job. Why can't I be myself outside of work? I should have the right to be me." That is true. We all have the right to be ourselves and do the things that make us happy. But life is a game and a very competitive one. The higher you want to go up the organizational ladder, the more you have to change. Remember Will Roger's quote: "When you're through changing, you are through." I don't think he was telling us we have to change our lives if we are happy with the life we are living. But I do think he is reminding us that life is a game, and there are many people who want that next upper-level position in your organization than just you. I think he is also reminding us that to remain competitive, you must be in a constant state of self-development. When you just want to stop your development and live the joys of life you currently have, it's okay to do so. What you can't expect is that all of your competitors will stop their development when you do. In this organizational game like any other, when you want to advance to the next higher league or level, there are dues that must be paid. One of the major dues that are required for upward mobility is the need to change and expand your life experiences.

We have seen it all of our lives. How many of your friends growing up dropped out of high school because they just didn't want to study, but you felt that the extra effort you displayed would get you to a higher level? In sports, you can see it being displayed by the high school basketball player that doesn't want to spend the extra time in the weight room or spend the time taking hundreds of hours perfecting their jump shot long after all other team members have left the gym and are enjoying pizza with their friends. Those pizza-loving friends may still want to advance to the next higher level, but in reality, they are not going to get a scholarship to that major university.

Executives often state that the people they are looking for are the folks that have "fire in their belly." Another way of saying this is, they are looking for people who are willing to pay the dues that will enable them to play at the next higher level in any activity in which they are engaged. Our careers demand the same commitment to growth, change, and the paying of the dues to advance to the next higher level in any organization. Remember, we have made the case in the P.I.E. Model, Performance is 10%. It merely gets you into the stadium and allows you to pay your current bills, but then the game begins for upward mobility.

IT'S JUST NOT THE RIGHT TIME

Timing in life is so important. Everyone must wait until the time is right for them to increase the intensity of their personal growth. A reason many hesitate to continue their self-improvement can be as simple as "I don't know if I really want to go to the next higher level." Why change your life if you haven't thought through if the dues you must pay are worth it? Remember you are changing from your current comfort zone to doing things that are new and uncomfortable for you. There is not much incentive to go through all of the aggravation if you really don't know if you want that upper-level position and lifestyle. This is the reason that career planning should really be called Life or Mutual Partner Planning when your career aspirations move beyond middle management.

The one observation I have made is that the rich and powerful who can do anything they want, seem to love playing golf, tennis, skiing, sailing, bridge, going to the symphony, ballet, and the many other activities of those upper-level. If those activities have lasted for hundreds of years, it might be possible that after trying some of them you might like them as well. The one thing that might be assured, we as individuals are not going to change those activities that the world's most powerful people are doing, simply because we don't like them.

SOLUTION: MAKE FAMILY AND SIGNIFICANT OTHERS INVOLVED IN A CAREER CHANGE

When you decide you want to grow your career to the next level, it might be important to think about and consider doing a few things. The first and maybe most important is to remember that this is your dream and career objective, not necessarily your partners. When you make that decision, you will be excited and committed to that dream. Your partner and or family may not be. It's not that they don't want to be supportive, but they may simply be busy defining their own life and goals.

That's fair for all parties, for if they don't pay attention to their life objectives, they can never reach them. As the old saying goes, "If you don't know where you are going, you might end up somewhere else." When they have established their goals, they, of course, will expect your support as well. In a partnership, both parties have a right to set their individual life objectives. So, when both have defined their definition of happiness with their careers and there is conflict, a happy compromise may be the best solution.

Everyone that has led a team or has been a manager of a department understands the importance of getting your team involved in the planning and making them aware of the mission of your unit. Getting every member of the team involved, promotes ownership of the mission and creates an environment where people are motivated to ensure the mission's success. Your significant other and family are no exception to those basic rules. Before this can be done, however, you have to decide where you want to take your career and be sure of your destination to be able to convince all to join you on your journey. Coming home one day and announcing to your family to pack because you just got a promotion to Fargo North Dakota without any upfront information might not turn out the way you expected or wanted. Life-changing information such as that, without fair warning to the parties that will be involved, will most likely be your toughest challenge to overcome when announcing your new promotion.

WHERE TO BEGIN—GET BUY-IN

Getting your significant other on board is essential. The earlier you can get them involved in your plans, the sooner they can work through their objections. Even better, is to allow them to be involved in your first thoughts of an upward career. However, even an earlier step may to prepare yourself for the objections they might have to your future career objectives. These might include such things as the impact that moving will have on your partner's future employment, your children's current school activities, everyone leaving their current friends and extended family members, and even a change in weather and locations such as moving from the beach to snow-covered mountains. The more prepared you are for what concerns they may have, the more effective you will be to help them address their concerns and turn some of them into benefits. Even if you do not have to move to another city for the first few promotions, just moving to a new home across town for an easier commute and thus the changing of schools, can be very traumatic for many children. But with your help, they will always survive.

WHAT'S IN IT FOR ME?

Many years ago, when I went to my first sales training, I was told that you can't sell anyone anything until you answer their basic question: "Why are we doing this?" And even more importantly, "If I do this, what's in it for me?" In essence, what benefits will be gained by the partner if he or she becomes supportive of your career objectives? Since they will quickly point out the negatives they will have for you making your career move, it will be up to you to point out the benefits they may gain by you moving your career to a higher level and/or to another city. Some of those benefits could include a higher salary that will help pay for some of the things the family might have wanted such as a used car for Jr. to drive to school, a family vacation to a place that was always out of your price range, a chance to go to a more expensive college of choice, a chance to ski every weekend if you are transferred closer to the mountains or the ability to spend more time at the beach if that location is in your future. There are benefits to every upward move that might balance out the personal changes that must be made by all. Everyone will be thinking about the negatives as well as they should. It will be up to you to research all the positives that the family will achieve if they buy in. As we are well aware, change of any kind can be very frightening for many people, so the more time you can give the people who will be affected by your advancement, the better they may be able to process the changes they will have to confront.

EXPLAINING THE RULES OF THE GAME- IS A GREAT PLACE TO START

In an earlier chapter, we explained that we are in a game that, if you are to be considered for upper-level positions, it might be required of you and your partner to learn and become involved in other lifestyle activities. Before springing on your partner that he or she has to learn golf or start going to the symphony, it might be helpful to explain the rules of the system to them. Let them know that the rules require high potential candidates to prepare themselves and their partners to adapt to a higher-level lifestyle in order to be effective in those higher-level positions. This might not be an issue for lower-level management positions, but it does apply to anyone desiring to move above those lower levels to middle management or a Junior executive position and above. Adaptation to the next higher lifestyle is necessary if one is to remain competitive with others who are making those changes.

Again, if you choose not to embrace the needed changes required for future advancement, it does not mean that you are a failure. It is also not an indicator that you won't be happy or even that you will not be able to make many major and meaningful contributions to your organization in the future. It just means that you no longer choose to compete for Jr. and Sr. executive positions that require you to interface comfortably with peers, customers, and the clients you will be working with at those upper levels. Explain to your partner that learning new activities and meeting new people are very much the same as paying the dues of getting a college degree that allowed you to advance to your current position. It simply boils down to asking your partner and yourself, "Do we want the things that upper and senior management positions can give us and our family, and are we willing to pay the dues required to reach those goals, or are we content and happy living our current life?"

GET BUY-IN FROM EVERYONE THAT WILL BE INVOLVED

It is important to get your partner to agree to help you on your journey to upward organizational positions. This help may come in the form of going to a company and/or community events that your attendants are required. It could also mean learning new activities and meeting new people. All of this means that your partner might have to step out of their comfort zone which can be very unnerving for them. Because of this, it may be important to remember that at these activities you will know some of the people who will be attending, and your partner may not have that luxury. Taking your partner to that event and just leaving them to fend on their own might not be the best strategy. Not for the best strategy. He or she will eventually connect with many members of your company but at the first few events, your support will be greatly appreciated. Your partner's understanding of why it is important for them to be there will go a long way to help them develop a positive attitude of support.

SLOW AND STEADY WINS THE RACE

The reality is, the dues that must be paid are very overrated. There is nothing that might be required of you to learn and if you choose to take on some of these new activities, you cannot get comfortable with within a very short period of time. As the expression goes, "It's not rocket science." Depending on the new activity you wish to learn and the motivation level you have to learn it, you can easily be a full participant in that activity in six months or less. At a minimum, you will be able to hold your own in any conversation about the subject when it occurs.

In one to two years, you can become so comfortable with the activity that you might be seen as, at a minimum, a person who has been doing it all of your life. Like learning a language, you will become fluent and not be intimidated participating in that activity with anyone. What you might experience is, the more competent you become with the new activity, the more fun it becomes. This fun usually leads to you wanting to do it more. Some activities might even become addictive, and you will make them one of your favorite things to do for the rest of your life. As an example, many people who first try to play golf come away from that experience touting it as a waste of time. If they stay with it, after a short period of time, they get hooked and can't get enough of it. Quilty!

One of the major reasons people get hooked on golf, tennis, bridge, skiing, musical theater, or other activities is because of the people they meet. Remember, "The game is about people" and many of your new activities will put you in contact with some great and exciting people that might become life-long friends. Some of these new folks will be knowledgeable on many subjects, and you can learn a lot from them. It is never too late to learn something new.

CHOOSING YOUR NEW ACTIVITIES

In choosing what new activities you might consider learning; two things should be considered. First and foremost, it should be something you and your partner would like to do or at least, an activity about which you have always been curious. A second consideration can come from you reading your environment and deciding what are the popular activities that the group members which you want to join are doing. Remember that once you learn a new activity, it will be something you can draw upon in discussions for the rest of your life, even though you don't have enough interest in that activity to continue your participation in it. Again, much of your continued interest will be based on the people you will meet as a result of participating in that activity.

You, of course, set the pace of your learning. It is entirely possible to learn several new activities at the same time. This would be the case if you combine physical activities like golf or tennis with learning about some of the arts such as the symphony or the ballet. Usually, the intensity of your learning will increase with your participation in that activity even to the level of taking lessons from a professional in the case of golf or tennis.

Learning a new activity does not always require a lot of money. For example, to cut down on the cost of learning golf, you can go to the local library to get free lessons from DVDs or books or even Google them. Once you learn the fundamental of a good golf swing, a visit to the local driving range, and the cost of a bucket of golf balls, you are off and running. Without much expense, you can discover if you like it or at a minimum, would have picked up enough about golf to enter into a golfing conversation at the neighborhood cocktail party. If your new activity is like learning bridge, again, just google it and you will be inundated with information. If you would like to learn how to have a formal dinner party, this is an area where you can try new dishes at home and have dress rehearsal dinners with family members or friends. With them, you can make mistakes with no embarrassing consequences, get great and honest feedback as to how to do it better next time, and at the same time, have a lot of fun.

WHEN CAN I STOP LEARNING?

The key is to keep learning and experiencing new things. I have often shared with young people that once they get their technical degree, they should understand that their learning in their lives is now about to begin. That rule applies to us older folks as well. It is never too old to start new things. When I tell people currently, I'm taking lessons in three different languages, they always ask why am I learning three languages at the same time at my age. My response is that I didn't learn them when I was their age.

One of my favorite stories concerns Pablo Casals, the world-class cellist, giving a concert at the Kennedy Center in Washington at the age of ninety-four. He was asked before the concert by a reporter, "I understand you still practice four hours every day. Is that true?" After saying yes, the reporter followed up with, "Why do you do that, everyone knows you're the greatest virtuoso the world has ever heard on the cello, plus you are ninety-four? His answer was very short and to the point. "I do it because I think I'm making progress." I was once told that if I didn't learn something new at least every six months, I would be coasting. And, if I was coasting, more than likely, I would be going downhill. Good advice for all of us. Always keep learning something new, if you do, you will not be coasting. Maybe it's time to act upon that statement we are always telling ourselves, "I've always wanted to... (fill in the blank)."

CONSIDER BEING A "JACK OF ALL TRADES"

My mother used to use the term Jack of all trades when she referred to a handyman that could fix just about anything that was broken but was not an expert on any given subject. I thought that was not a good thing when I learned that the saying ended with "and master of none." I concluded that it was far better to stick with one activity until you were the best at it. That meant that you had conquered at least something in which no one could beat you. After all, our sports heroes are the people who stand alone at the pinnacle of their sport. Babe Ruth, Hank Aaron, and Muhammad Ali were not number two people. They were the very best and that is why they were idolized. So, a logical conclusion might be to not spread yourself around learning a lot of things, just get really good at one.

I'd like to give a counter viewpoint. That is, maybe learning a little about a lot of things might have its advantages. The first and foremost advantage you might have is the number of different people you will have the opportunity to meet. Since the game is about people and every new activity that you learn will put you into a group of new people, it will automatically expand your personal network. Also, every new activity will dictate new experiences, new challenges, new insights, and a broadening of your perspectives.

A word of caution. You should make sure that when you take on a new activity, you stay with it until you reach the "Jack" level and not stop your growth in that new activity at the fifth or sixth levels in the deck. That is to say, as my father often reminded me, "Harvey, if you're going to do something, do it right." When you take on a new activity, make sure you stay with it until you can say, "I can hold my own" in that activity. You might not want to dedicate the time to become one of the world's best but as you meet people along your journey, you will be able to be respected for your knowledge, experience, or skill in the activity that is in question. You might not be the world's best but if you are better than ninety percent of the people at the Friday night cocktail party, that is probably all you need. When you meet one of the ten percent individuals that are better than you, it becomes a great learning session for you if you are open to listening and learning. Finally, learning and participating in many activities can be fun. It can take a life that might fall into routines and even ruts, to being one of excitement and challenges. Even activities that you tried many years ago can prove to be beneficial to you later in life. This happened to me with ballet.

When I was twelve years old and would ride my bike to baseball practice, I had to pass this dance studio with a big glass window. My curiosity was aroused when I first saw the dance class of about twenty young girls my age in their tutus going through their dance routines. When I stopped and observed the class for the third or fourth time, the ballet instructor beckoned me to come in and asked if I wanted to try. To ask a twelve-year-old if he wanted to spend an hour being the only boy with twenty girls was a no-brainier for me. I quickly learned ballet's five positions and was well on the way to trading my future baseball fame for my newly founded dance career. I was Billy Elliot.

This, however, was in 1952, I was "Colored", all the girls were White and it took four months before their parents demanded that I be thrown out of the class. However, those four months were enough for me to get the bug about ballet and appreciate its difficulty and artistic expression. That stayed with me in my adult life when traveling to cities all over the world, I would make it a point to see the great ballet companies which included The New York ballet, The San Francisco Ballet, The American Ballet, The Royal Ballet, The Bolshoi Ballet and many more. I then became a season ticket holder to my hometown ballet, The Atlanta Ballet (one of the best in the country if not the world). Sixty-eight years after my first ballet lesson I was at a community benefit dinner and sat beside one of the administrators of the Atlanta Ballet. The great conversation we had about ballet led to an invitation to join the Atlanta Ballet Board of Advisors. I give credit to this honor happening to me because when I was twelve, I took a chance in trying something new by going in when that ballet instructor beckoned and sparked an interest that has stayed with me for the rest of my life. I did not become a master but I'm very happy that I became a "Jack" and made ballet one of my "trades."

CHAPTER ELEVEN

THE DYNAMICS OF CULTURE

CULTURE IS BAKED IN; IT IS A PART OF WHO YOU ARE

In the more than fifty years I have been training Women and Minority Internal Resource Groups, I have observed the most difficult issues that confront a great number of my participants is the fear of losing their cultural identity if they chose to play "the game." I wish I could report that after fifty years that challenge for maintaining ones cultural, racial or gender identity has greatly reduced, but I cannot. In the training classes I am currently conducting, this is still a major issue with many.

To examine this issue effectively, maybe it would be good to review the definition of culture. It is "a set of beliefs, customs, traditions, language, and values that have been passed from generation to generation." This of course would include the racial cultures (Black, White, Asian, Hispanic, Indigenous), and all ethnic cultures which would include such groups as Italian American, Irish American, German American, and Polish American and the list could fill out the page. We could then add to this list religious' cultures such as Jewish, Moslem, Protestant, Buddhist, and so on. Of course, within all of these cultures, there is the subculture of gender and age.

A major culture that is often overlooked is all of the socio-economic cultures we have in our society. We are all born into a socioeconomic level which is the level of our parents. This can range from an underclass, working class, professional class, executive class, or old money environments. It is easy to see that all of us are made up of several different cultures that are blended into who we are. These different cultures might consist of race, religion, ethnicity, sexual orientation and as we have just suggested, our socioeconomic backgrounds. If you want to determine your native cultural roots, just review the environments you were exposed to from birth to eighteen years of age. The environments you were exposed to and lessons you learned during those years are baked in. This determines who you are and you will remain so until you make the effort to change yourself. If you do not make that effort, more than likely you are that same person you were at eighteen. You do not lose your culture; it is the core of who you are. You might add to that core as you gain other life experiences, but that core will always be there and you can call on it whenever needed.

It is also important to understand that any culture can be learned by anyone who chooses to do so. How fast this can be done will depend on our motivational level to learn a different culture outside of our native culture, as well as the amount of exposure we have to that culture. To take French lessons once a week without any reinforcement outside of that once-a-week lesson, the learning process to become fluent (to be able to speak a language without consciously thinking about every word that's said), might take a decade or maybe never be accomplished. However, if you moved to France and could not speak a word of French but keeping your new position depended upon you speaking French fluently, it is possible to become fluent in a relatively short period of time. The same is true for any cultural group that we have listed. With the right motivation and access, any one of us can become fluent in any of those upper-level socio-economic cultures in a short period of time as well. As our parents told us "You do become the person with whom you surround yourself."

THE ADVANTAGE OF BECOMING FLUENT IN OTHER CULTURES

It can't be said enough, "the game is about people and everything else is detail." This simply means that any success we might have in our lives will be based on what other people will share with or give us. All promotions raise, and critical assignments that will happen in our careers will come from another person. Even self-employed individuals understand that every sale they make comes from a person. How we connect with other individuals is really important and can affect our careers and lives. With that said, it is not hard to imagine that, when given a choice of rewarding an individual that you are uncomfortable versus comfortable with, more than likely the person with whom you are most comfortable will get that reward.

Fluency in the culture in which you are involved is simply one of the ways people can gain your trust and become comfortable being around you. From a language perspective, we all might have an experience with that person who is just learning English, and we must pull every other word from them. We are impressed by the fact that he or she is learning another language but every conversation we have with them is work. Just for no other reason, we try to avoid that individual to simply cut down on the stress that a conversation with them can cause. Fluency in any language or culture helps relationships.

IS "CODE-SWITCHING" A VIABLE OPTION?

A new term that is being used by some younger workers is "code-switching." This is when a person in their organization has a different language and set of actions for whites in the organization versus their (as an example) Black associates. The argument for justifying the use of code-switching is that it allows other blacks to identify with each other and will ease the stress of always having to step into other people's worlds all day long. It's the "Black lunch table scenario" where one feels that they should have at least one hour a day to relax with a few people with whom they are comfortable.

Of course, the downside to this is obvious. The message that is sent may be negatively interpreted by some people observing this behavior. For one, it may be translated that you are not as professional or comfortable with the business culture as you should be. As we indicated business is a language and has a unique culture of its own. This culture is usually the bases for judging if a person is professional or not. Being observed by potential sponsors that you break from business norms to your personal cultural norms may give the message that you are not entirely committed to the business culture and thus your career. If a competitor of yours is seen as more committed, they will usually win that person's sponsorship.

How would it be perceived by the English-speaking people in a department if two Mexican associates were always talking in Spanish when they got together in front of their English-speaking teammates? Oh, some may say it doesn't bother them but many others may wonder why their Hispanic team members were always separating themselves from the team. It gets worse if one is in a leadership role and must pass out assignments and raises to team members. If so, they should prepare themselves to be accused of favoritism whenever they rightfully give a deserved reward to one of the associates with which they talk in code-switching. Everyone will believe that the decision was not made on a fair basis. It might also be interpreted by a potential sponsor that you might not be able to manage a diverse department moving forward.

CAN I KEEP MY CULTURE OR MUST I BECOME A "SELL-OUT?"

Words can be hurtful and extremely harmful. None more so than being labeled with the phrase "selling out." Most people have so much pride in their cultural background that the one thing they never want to hear from a member of their racial group is that they have turned their back on their race. As a result, people know they can use the term "selling out" to keep other members of their group from expanding their world and broadening themselves. To express it in other terms, it is one of the great weapons to keep all crabs in the barrel. It is usually administrated by the crab that has decided to stay in the barrel and doesn't want anyone else to leave what I'm calling their cultural, racial, or religious reservation.

The core reason that this often occurs is the fear of change. It occurs when a person is confronted with the need to break away from the comfortable activities they have practiced all of their life in order to move their career ahead. The new requirements are strange ones and with their lack of fluency, they become uncomfortable and may even resent having to distance themselves from family and friends. You can see why someone in that position might be easily persuaded to give up trying to learn those new skills. Why risk being labeled a sell-out with your current set of friends when there is no guarantee that by learning those new activities, you will be successful in that strange new environment?

CAN I BE AN EXCEPTION TO THE RULES?

Sorry, the rules that are in place apply to every individual, every cultural group, every organization, and even every nation. The only question that any of those entities have to answer is "Do I want to play?" You see, the only way the business game can work is to have rules. Without rules, the global economy would crumble into total disarray and chaos. The rules are the same for everyone and have been in place for hundreds of years. If you decide you want to play your organization's game and want your career to be upwardly oriented, you are going to experience personal change many times in your career. The organization is not going to change for you, you must decide what level of the organization to which you want to make your contribution, and then adapt to that level.

BUT I'M PROUD OF MY CULTURE

Having pride in your cultural background is not unique to any one race or ethnic group, but all have had to leave behind many of their cultural comforts and traditions when they enter mainstream America. The first or second-generation Italian American who moves out of "Little Italy" must leave that environment with its rich cultures when they move into the entry professional levels of business. A person who has parents that still live in Chinatown, the Korean, Irish, and German communities all experience a sense of loss and an abandonment of their culture when they break from their perspective communities. This process, of course, becomes easier the greater the number of generations that have passed since the family first left their cultural community. As an African-American, I often hear from members of my race that they feel we are the only ones in the game that have to give up elements of our culture. This is just not true. Many of the earlier immigrants into our system even went as far as to change their family names to become more mainstream. As mentioned before, you will rarely hear someone labeled as white, correct that label by saying, "No

I'm not white, I'm Italian." They have pride in their background but don't feel the need to be totally defined by it. This is a major step for anyone wanting to succeed in mainstream America.

THEN ...... "WHO AM I?"

Many former and great philosophers have asked and pondered that question for thousands of years. Although I don't fall into that august group, I have thought about that question. My conclusion is that I am a person of many entities which are in a constant state of change. Some of those entities include my gender, my race, my role as a husband, a father, a friend, my profession, my socioeconomic level and so many more. But outside of my race and gender, the other entities are in a constant state of change. They are continually changing in priority as well as how effective I am in any of those roles at any given time. If you don't believe me, just ask my wife regarding my role as a husband. I'm sure her opinion of me as a great husband has changed many times over our sixty years of marriage. I often think that sometimes we define ourselves into a box, put our feet in buckets of cement, and feel that we cannot or should not have to ever redefine ourselves.

As we experience more of life and gain more knowledge, it is natural to allow those life experiences to redefine how we think, our beliefs, and what we feel is important. I also feel that our definition of ourselves does not have to be so rigid that it can only encompass only one role at a time. Why can't I be a husband, father, professional, and a black man all at the same time? As to which one takes priority at any given time is a moving target and all the entities that define who we are must be managed by each individual. "I am not the man or woman I used to be" is a valid statement that almost any person can make. It just says that we are all works in progress and that if I lock into place my permanent definition of "who I am," I will more than likely stunt my future growth by not being open to change. An example for me is, I was once a bowler and was very proud of my 195 bowling average. I am now a golfer, tennis player, and skier. I once was a Doo-wop singer but now love musical theater, ballet, and opera. Change often requires that we must let go of some old things to be able to embrace new challenges and life experiences.

LETTING GO—THE DIFFICULTY OF CHANGE

One of the observations I experienced early in my life growing up in a predominantly Italian neighborhood that had many immigrant families, was the willingness many people had to join the mainstream. Specifically, I remembered seeing one of my friends being slapped on the back of his head by his father when he said something in Italian with a follow-up statement, "You are in America, you speak English." This along with witnessing families changing their last names to make them more "American" made me realize the extent that people would go through to better fit into the American mainstream. Even today, we see second and third-generation Italians who have left their communities and are still very proud of their ethnic ancestry. But in spite of their ethnic pride, they have no problem being referred to as "just an American." For that person, being Italian is still very much a part of who he is but they also are not totally defined by that important part of their life.

If I learn all of these mainstream activities, am I forsaking my culture?

Remember, one of the basic rules of the system is whoever is at the top of any pyramid has the right to make the rules. When England was at the top of the global system, it defined the rules that the world plays by today. The fact that the world speaks English, plays golf, tennis, sail, and plays games involving the horse such as polo and fox hunting, all is because England said the world will participate in these activities, and indeed the world does just that. To confirm this, all we have to do is look at the world's participation in the next U.S. Open Tennis or Golf tournaments. Every major nation has representatives who are participating. This just shows that the game is global, and there are specific activities that are available to anyone who wants to participate in "the game" at the higher levels on the world stage.

The point to consider is, a person might be limiting themselves if they categorize activities as being black or white. It also is not recognizing the great contributions that African-Americans and other people of color have made in those arenas that are considered upper socio-economic activities. If a person can expand their mind to be more accepting of other activities and begin to participate in them, they also can expand the possibilities of moving their life and career into upper-level positions. The factors that will control that possibility are the desire to want it, the willingness to pay the dues of learning about them, and the courage to try new adventures. Doing so just may change your life. The one thing that I can almost guarantee is that learning any of those activities will not make you less Black or less any other cultural group in which you have great pride and identification. It also will allow you to take pride in the many contributions that have been made by members of your race and ethnic background in all of those "white" activities. They deserve to be recognized and honored.

IS IT CULTURE, FASHION, OR FAD?

Of course, we all are proud of our various cultures and want to preserve and participate in their richness. But we must be careful not to mistake cultural values with things that fall into the category of fashion or fads. To ensure that this does not happen, let's review the definition of culture once more. Remember, it is something that is passed on from generation to generation. I experienced a situation many years ago that put this issue to the test. It was a time when young Black and Hispanic workers started to carve their names, initials, and symbols on the back of their heads. After giving a presentation in this major Fortune 500 corporation, a senior officer asks if I had time to have lunch with a young Black employee that he described as high potential and was highly thought of within the company. He then followed up with a major concern he had. That concern was he had his name, Carl, carved into the back of his head and felt that it was not looked upon as positive. He was afraid that it might affect his future upward mobility and felt he should be told. He stated he was going to do it but felt it might be taken better coming from me. His request points out why many women and people of color often do not get the important information that could help their career growth because many potential mentors that are white are afraid to share information that might make them appear racist.

Sitting down with Carl, I explain to him that he was shaking up the management team with his name carved into his head. Carl quickly went on the defensive by explaining to me that the organization was simply closed-minded and maybe a little racist by not allowing him to practice his culture. With a slight smile, I asked a very obvious question which was, "You do know Carl that I am African-American?" When he responded in the affirmative, I continued. "Carl, I want you to know I am very proud of my African-American heritage." Carl, I continued, "I want you to also know (wanting to inject a little levity into the conversation) I have been an African- American all of my life." Then I followed with my closer. "And you should also know Carl that I have never had 'Harv' carved into the back of my head." And after a few more months, neither did Carl.

Carl had confused culture with a current fashion statement or a fad that he and his African-Americans friends had decided was a fun thing to do. Having his name carved into the back of his head did not pass the test of something that had been passed on from generation to generation. When the fad faded, so did his name from the back of his head.

What then can be claimed as cultural values that should be guarded, defended, practiced, and passed on to others? Well, who has not heard from their parents that you should "Do your best," "Work hard," "Be kind and giving to other people," "Take pride in yourself and everything that you do," "Never give up even if you are knocked down," and of course, "Do unto others as you would have them do unto you." Those are the cultural values that have been passed down to us that we should never forget and never stop practicing. The great thing about those values is that more than likely, those are also the values of your organization. They are delighted when anyone displays those cultural values at work and will be delighted if you practice those values for the length of your employment.

As far as fads and fashions are concerned, organizations are trying to become tolerant about allowing them as long as they do not affect the productivity of the team. This is particularly true for people in entry-level positions. The reasoning is two-fold. One is if you are new to the organizational culture and recently just left or still living in your racial or ethnic culture, you may need time to make adjustments before embracing the business culture. The organizational culture also assumes that everyone does not want upward advancement, and if an employee doesn't have daily customer contact or their attire is not disruptive and does not affect the bottom line, more flexibility and tolerance can be shown at that level of the organization. It is when an individual is competing for a higher-level position that might require a leadership role and is a position where they will be representing the organization to the outside world, it might be expected that one should become more comfortable with the business cultural requirement of that higher level. At those higher levels that require customer contact, you are representing the organization, not just yourself and the organization (since it is paying the bills) can expect a person in those higher positions to display organizational values. This may mean showing less of one's culture on the job. After all, as a manager in a multi-cultural workforce, you are expected to relate and communicate effectively with people of many different cultures. At this point, the business culture becomes the common culture or language for all. The values you can bring from your native culture are the perspectives, experiences, and lessons you have been taught from childhood. Wearing your culture on your sleeve might not be the most effective strategy if you want to reach the C-suite. But don't worry, when you get to the C-suite you will meet a lot of other people who will have made the same choices about their culture as you have done.

BUT AGAIN, IT'S JUST NOT FAIR

There can be a good case made by some that the rules of the game are just not fair since the rules were made by men who were English and who had wealth and power. In today's world, if you have parents who were executives and you went to a private school that taught you all of the activities of upper-level society, you clearly have a running head start and thus an advantage. If you do not fall into that category and you feel bad about your fate, my only advice is to "just get over it." That's how it is, and it will always be that way. The positive element is that the game today allows everyone to play and we have all seen that people of all cultures have risen to the top of their organization if they are willing to accept the rules and play by them. If you think about it, there can never be a set of rules that would be equal for everyone. As we mentioned before, in your current situation, would you change it with a disabled gay, lesbian or transgender person. How about a first-generation immigrant that has yet to master English? This is a list that could go on for pages. You can never have a set of rules that will be fair for everyone. We all must play with the cards we have been dealt in life. The key is, the rules allow anyone to compete in this game and be able to overcome any disadvantage with which they might have started.

A great quote from the famous golfer Bobby Jones upon learning he had a terminal illness stated that "Life is like golf; you play it as it lies." That very much describes all of our lives and careers. There is no value in complaining about our situation in life. Maybe a better approach is to accept where life has defined our starting point and just do our very best from where we are; remembering that many people have started with far greater handicaps and have moved on to make impactful contributions to their lives and others.

This can be done if they are given the rules and if they want to play by those rules badly enough. We have seen so many people do just that. When our parents told us that life is not fair, I concluded that if the system would let me in to compete, I would play hard and let my results determine if I'm good enough.

The cultural value that has always been the foundation of my motivation was passed on to me by my father, as he stood in front of the window watching the burning cross, telling me to never let anyone keep me from doing what I wanted to do in life.

CHAPTER TWELVE

LOOKING BACK, GOING FORWARD: *THE AFRICAN-AMERICAN JOURNEY TO MAINSTREAM AMERICA*

The topics to be discussed in this chapter apply to all cultures but with your permission, I would like to discuss some of the next issues from my personal experiences and from the lenses of my African-American culture. This information is not aimed to be critical of any past actions that we as a race have taken or to cast blame on past strategies we have used and are currently using. As a community, we have done what we had to do and must continue to concentrate on what must be done to obtain a level playing field in our country. We must be constant with our pursuit to gain equality in all areas of American life. The fight must continue in the courts, the legislatures, the media, and the peaceful protesting that is occurring in our streets. However, a question that should be discussed is "What's next?" It's a good question that we African-Americans should be asking ourselves as we seek equal justice in the many areas that are currently being highlighted by current protests. Some progress and changes I'm sure will happen. However, we can safely assume, according to past history, none of these issues will be totally resolved. Power is very reluctant to relinquish any more of its power than is necessary.

We, as a people, have been asking the system to give us **more** for hundreds of years. These requests have ranged from "free us from slavery," "allow us to vote," "stop lynching us" to "give us equality in the areas of criminal justice, housing, health care," and the list goes on. However, before addressing the question of "What's next?" The question of "What if?" Should be put on the table for discussion. What if we do achieve equal treatment in all areas of our society? What do we do next? What efforts have we made in preparing this and future generations to make the most effective use of our new freedoms and equalities when they finally arrive?

The mainstream game is a competitive one, and any future gains will be won by individuals, not as a group. While still pursuing the issue of equality as a group, it is time as individuals to decide if they want to compete in the mainstream system if that equality happens. Or maybe more importantly, what should we do if that equality never comes in our lifetime? I have compared our current situation to a man or woman standing on the bank of a swift-flowing river knowing that if they jump into the river, it will take them where they want to go. The only reason they may be hesitant is that they do not know how to swim.

There is a viable solution for us as African-Americans that will take us to our next level of progress. It's simple. Just learn how to swim in mainstream America. In my research, I have been able to figure out how our system works and can provide that information. It is information that will allow more of us as African-Americans to have the confidence to commit ourselves to play in the American system.

Of course, many African-Americans have successfully played and are currently playing the "mainstream game" effectively in spite of not having a level playing field. Their contributions have helped make great gains for our community and for the entire nation. But to change from having to ask for more to ensuring that it happens, we need to be in enough power positions to help make the rules and oversee the fair administration of those rules.

For this to occur, we **must** learn the rules of the mainstream system and then become efficient at playing by them. We now need to exercise the freedoms for which we have fought and died since the passage of the thirteenth amendment that freed us and the 1964 Civil Rights Act that allowed us to enter the mainstream game. Far too many of us are still standing on the bank of the river looking at opportunity flow by.

AFRICAN-AMERICANS AND THE AMERICAN MAINSTREAM

Our history of great mainstream players goes back not only to famous contributors such as Fredrick Douglas but also to lesser-known past effective mainstream players which include many of our fathers and mothers. We have proven that despite the barriers, we can play the mainstream game successfully. We have advanced to positions of Senators, Governors, Ambassadors, Generals, CEO's of Fortune 500 companies, heads of major government agencies, Presidential cabinet positions, and yes, even capturing the highest position in our country, President of the United States. We know it can be done. We must now combine our protesting with a full-scale effort to get more of our community to become competitive players in mainstream America. We must change the perspective of it being **THEIR** mainstream to it being **OUR** mainstream.

Looking at history, we as African-Americans have hit another "**glass ceiling**." I say another because it has happened many times before. As a race, our progress and changes can be reflected in the racial titles we have adopted. We have gone from Slaves to Colored People to Negro to Black to Afro-American to African-American to People of Color. Each of those name identifications represents a "glass ceiling" that had to be mentally broken through in order to make advancement possible as a race. We are currently facing another and hopefully the last glass ceiling we must penetrate. However, to do so will require a major shift in perspectives and attitudes.

The first major change that occurred in our history was to be freed as slaves and recognized as "Colored People." This change allowed us to be viewed for the first time as people and not be considered property. The next major change was when we started to find our racial identity with the title of Negro. During this period, we stepped away from society's label of just being "Colored" and redefined ourselves as having a specific identity, history, and rich culture. We felt that the term "Negro" gave us a greater sense of ownership and definition as to whom we thought we were. We advanced those feelings when we adopted the term "Black" and told ourselves and the world that Black was beautiful.

The next glass ceiling breakthrough was a major step on our journey because, although still recognizing our uniqueness as a people by defining ourselves as "Afro" and more recently "African," we made a major addition to those words by adding "American" to those titles. It was a major step in recognizing that we do belong in the mainstream of this country and wanted no longer to be left out. The latest title identification, "People of Color" brings us very close to where we began as "Colored People."

Understanding that this label is meant to include other racial groups, the major concern is that the term American was dropped. With this latest designation, we have stalled in our journey to become a part of the "American" mainstream. It seems that we are caught in a loop still trying to find our place in the American system. We are still on the outside looking in. The result is that we are still expecting the system to make progress for us instead of taking control of our own destiny. We must stop claiming to be "victims of our system" (which of course we are) and making our case from a defensive posture. If we continue this strategy, I'm afraid our journey will continue to be a very slow one. Our nation's history has shown us how slow the system is open to changing and leveling the playing field for all. Fortunately, our talented Black youth (as well as young people from all races) are telling this nation that they are no longer willing to wait.

The only next logical option is to take on the responsibility of "Empowering" ourselves and reaching our personal objectives through our own talents and abilities. For this to be accomplished, there must first be a recognition that there is a "Mainstream America" and second that there is a "Game" that is being played. The term "Game" requires the understanding that we are in a competitive system made up of specific "unwritten rules" that define how it operates.

For any individual to take control of their destiny, they must first decide that they want to leave the African-American "reservation" and step into the Mainstream. Our reservation is not just physical like the ones in which we placed Native Americans, for many African-Americans our reservation is a mental one and is of our own choosing. Until a person comes to that recognition and commits to learning the rules of the American mainstream game, they will never make the progress they desire. We have heard the expression "You can't play any game effectively if you don't know the rules of the game you are playing." I have found this to be true with many African-Americans as it relates to mainstream America. If this was a military battle and we were defining our strategy, it has been to fight merely a defensive war instead of developing an aggressive offensive strategy that I feel we must now add to our defensive past.

If we are to win, we must now live up to the "American" in our African-American label by leaving the "mental reservation" we often imposed on ourselves and stop avoiding participating in mainstream America. Instead, we must start to aggressively play the mainstream game that contains the rewards we say we want to share. This can be done by putting ourselves into the mainstream where we can allow our talents to grow and flourish. After all, isn't that the freedom for which we fought so hard and for which so many people dedicated their lives and even died? We are, of course, not the only culture in our country that has "mental reservations." They can be found in "Little Italy," Germantown, Chinatown, the Jewish community, or any group of people who find it comfortable to live around familiar settings and be with people they currently enjoy.

There should be no judgment made on anyone's decision to choose the life they want to live. For example, unlike Native Americans, a white Italian living in "Little Italy" has no physical or legal restrictions that keep him or her there. It is their choice to either stay in their Italian community or ventures out into mainstream America. Whatever their choice may be (a choice of which they have 100% control), if they want to succeed in either, they must play by the rules of that specific environment. Since both environments are competitive ones, it will be very difficult to beat competitors in either environment if you are not totally committed to that specific environment. There is an "unwritten rule" that tells us "You can't always be all things to all people." To me, that simply says, by giving both environments only fifty percent of your time, commitment, and/or effort, it will be very difficult to defeat anyone that is giving ninety percent effort to either one.

So, what would motivate a member of any group who puts their current identification in a race, gender, immigrant status, sexual orientation, or religion but still wants to seek out the mainstream environment? How do we get those who are standing on the bank of the river too intimidated to jump in but knowing if they do, that river can take them to where they want to go? I have found the solution to be very simple and obvious. **We should just give a person the knowledge and understanding of the rules of the mainstream American game.** In essence, teach them how to swim. That is what my **P.I.E. Model** will do. This model will be explained in more detail in a later chapter. The Model helps a person understand that learning and practicing the mainstream business rules is not selling out one's culture. We usually admire people whose native language is English, and they master a second foreign language. This is not true when a person ventures out of his or her native culture. There is tremendous pressure in those "cultural reservations" to keep their members from leaving. The label of "selling out" or being an "Uncle Tom" is for many, a barrier too difficult to overcome.

The fact is, there is no "it's them or us" in the business culture. Whether it is communicating with someone on a global level or within their own company, the rules are the same for everyone. This would include an Italian, a woman, an African-American, or a transgender. As individuals, we all have a choice regarding the level of commitment we wish to give to the rules of the various environments in which we live. However, if anyone is to make an informed decision with regards to which game they want to play, the rules must be shared with that individual. It is important to show that anyone who wants to share in the rewards of mainstream America can have them, but to do so they must eventually embrace the mainstream rules no matter who they are. There are no exceptions. Knowing this makes accepting the rules much easier. A person's degree of success is directly related to the degree that they commit to learning and playing by the rules effectively. However, if they are motivated to leave their mental reservation state of mind, they will become greater contributors to any organization's missions as well as becoming better candidates for future leadership positions.

It cannot go unnoticed that in every game African-Americans have been allowed to play. We instantly start to contribute and in time, soon become a dominating force. This has happened in such areas as baseball, football, basketball, and music, just to name a few. Even the activities that we have entered into in very few numbers, many of those people have ended up at the very top of all competitors. This can be seen with Tiger Woods in golf and the Williams sisters in tennis. They have achieved their accomplishments, of course, with talent and dedication. The one constant in all of these areas is that they learned how those games must be played in order to win. You have to learn the rules to play any game well. We have not learned the rules of the organizational game and as a result, have not had the large numerical successes and accomplishments we have enjoyed in the other games we have entered.

For the last forty years, I have researched the "unwritten rules" of our system and how they dictate the way a person can improve their job position, as well as their socio-economic status. It is critical knowledge that needs to be exposed to every working American, especially to women, people of color, the emerging immigrant population, and any other individual that was raised outside of the mainstream.

It is also especially important that the rules be shared with our children for their future career success. I have published three books, with this being my fourth. All of them cover the topic of upward mobility and how, what I call "the game," must be played to achieve advancement to a higher position and/or socio-economic level.

In those forty years of writing down the "unwritten rules," I have also been teaching these rules in seminars geared toward women, minorities, white managers, and executives. Of the tens of thousands of people with which I have shared my information, many have advanced to high positions and almost everyone who hears the rules, have told me knowing them has changed their lives. Just recently, the Chief Human Resources Officer for a major Fortune 500 company and an African-American, saw me in the parking lot of an Atlanta Mall and told me that he had taken my training twenty years ago and that it changed his entire career strategy and it was one of the major reason he was in his job today. When people understand the rules of our system, it becomes a powerful motivator to put into action, strategies that allow them to move their careers forward.

When we hear a person state, "You gotta play the game." Rarely if ever, do the rules needed to play this "game" follow that statement. Uncovering, learning, practicing, and teaching these rules is what I have chosen as my life's work. The future progress of women and people of color should not be on the shoulders of Human Resources. When future leadership growth is put in the hands of every individual, that is when large numbers from all population groups will start to emerge as leaders.

THE ROAD TO THE MAINSTREAM FOR ASIAN AND LATINX AMERICANS

As I stated before, my thoughts in this book emanate from my native culture of being African-American and the experiences I have had with other cultures. I also have had the pleasure of facilitating classes of Women, Black, Asian, Hispanic, and Gay/Lesbian Employee Resource Groups for over forty-five years. This experience has taught me the similarities that all people of color and women have on their journey to mainstream America.

For Asian and Hispanic alike, both groups had to go through periods of extreme prejudice having been inflected on them by not only American citizens but by national legislation as well. It is important to remind ourselves that although we lump these citizens into two groups (Asian and Hispanic), they represent many proud cultural communities. Asian would include such citizens and immigrants as Japanese, Chinese, Korean, Vietnamese, and many others. Latinx would include such citizens and immigrants as Mexican, Cuban, Puerto Rican, and again many other Spanish-speaking cultures.

Although the history of immigrating to America differs for each culture, a great number of Chinese and Mexican immigrants enter in the mid-1800s to help with mining gold and building the railroad. When that was exhausted, many relocated to large west coast cities and started their cultural reservations. Koreans,

Filipinos, and Japanese largely came as refugees from wars in Asia. Many immigrated to Hawaii and west coast cities as well. Cubans and Puerto Ricans settled in South Florida. Many Japanese and Puerto Ricans became citizens when Hawaii became a state and Puerto Rico became a U.S. territory.

All groups had to go through the "second class citizens" experience and periods of extreme prejudicial treatment. National and State laws were passed to ban the immigration of Chinese and Japanese citizens were put into internment camps during World War II. Societal violence has always been a factor in all of those communities' histories and we can see that much of it still remains. A particular show of racial prejudice can be seen in the spike in harassment and even violence toward Asian citizens since Covid-19. This is another indicator that skin color makes a difference. Those perpetrating harassment and violence toward our fellow citizens that are Chinese don't bother to find out if they are Chinese or not, anyone that is Asian for them is close enough. It is important, as Americans, to remind ourselves that all of these groups have made enormous contributions to our nation while struggling on their journeys to equal citizenship and their personal American Dream.

At this point, I think it is fair to say that all races and genders have the same challenges to get into mainstream America. Of course, at any given period, any one group may be more out of favor than any other but that is not the major issue. The fact is as I explained from my Black American perspective, an Asian or Hispanic individual must also learn and play by the mainstream rules if they are to succeed in the American mainstream.

CHAPTER THIRTEEN

WOMEN AND THEIR JOURNEY TO THE MOUNTAIN TOP

SO, WHAT DO I KNOW ABOUT THE WOMEN'S JOURNEY?

I am a man about to make some observations about women and their struggle to be accepted as equals in our society. The first question that should be asked of me is, "Who made you an authority on women?" Speaking on behalf of all men, none of us can nor ever will be an authority on the female culture. It is much too complicated and every woman, like snowflakes, is unique and has her own style, beauty, and individuality. If, however, being a close observer of the women's culture and even taking on some of the challenges with which women are confronted, hopefully, might allow me to at least make a few comments.

My qualifications start with being raised by a woman and what a woman my mother was. Strong and supportive of her children and my father, we looked to her for guidance and strength the entire time she was with us. She not only kept our home in order but also worked alongside my father in our family's restaurant business. Since I had three brothers and no sisters, all the home chores, normally relegated in the forties and fifties to girls, were placed squarely on our shoulders. This included washing dishes and clothes, ironing, sewing, and helping with the cooking.

This was of great help to me later in my life when I was a househusband after my wife and I had our first son. I had just left the Army and was preparing to go back to school to complete my degree. My wife was a teacher, and it fell upon me to keep our house, cook meals, take care of the baby, and generally duplicate the actions of my mother. I remember making sure that I fed Kevin, my son, every day at noon so that I could watch General Hospital and Search for Tomorrow. The dilemma I had at the Friday night neighborhood parties was deciding, do I talk with the guys about the football games or the wives about what was going on in my Soaps. I also remember the frustration when I would cook dinner and my wife would get home late. I always wanted my meals to be served at their best.

My greatest experience in the women's culture came when I was hired by Boyle-Kirkman and Associates, the first women's consulting firm that was founded in our country, located in the Chrysler Building in New York City. I was the only man among thirty-two women and worked there for three years. I mentioned before that it takes two to three years to become fluent in any culture and that experience got me as close to fluency in the women's culture as I think a man can ever get.

How that came about was back in the late sixties. I helped to write IBM's first Black Awareness program, the first corporation to do so in the country. Also, the first Women's Awareness program was developed by Barbara Boyle and Sharon Kirkman. They received so many inquiries as to what they were doing that they decided to start their own consulting firm. However, it was during the rioting of the seventies that companies were asking for help with their Black issues and they asked me to join them. Our company was so unique at the time that 60 minutes gave us a twenty-minute segment on their show. No one could believe that any organization would actually bother training women to be managers. It was widely believed at that time, women could never manage men and thus training them to be managers was a waste of both time and money.

After I became "one of the girls," I had three years to hear the struggles my associates had with gender bias and the relationships they had with husbands, boyfriends, and men in general. When

I left that firm to start my own business, it took me at least six months to begin liking men again. This was during the Women's Revolution of the seventies and being in New York, I had a chance to meet some of the great leaders of that movement including Betty Friedan, Gloria Steinem, and Helen Curley Brown. I recall one of the great fun moments we had as a firm, was when Billy Jean King beat Bobby Riggs in their now classic tennis match. Of course, I was on team Billy Jean.

Another opportunity I have had to understand women's journey toward equal acceptance is to have conducted seminars for professional women for forty years. This has allowed me to witness not only the transition of our organizational cultures to be more open to accepting the talents that women can bring to the organizational table, but also see the change in perception and attitudes of the women's culture during this period as well. Early concerns of women ranged from trying to get their husband's help with the home, to get them more supportive of their career ambitions, to even hiding how much money they were making from their husbands in order to not make them feel less inferior and more manly.

I think it might be fair to say, that we men have come a long way to becoming more helpful and supportive of women at home and with their career ambitions but still, many of us have a way to go. My last qualification is that Kita, my wife of sixty years, has not thrown me out...Yet. I have ducked, dodged, avoided, and survived all the mistakes I've made in marriage so far and it looks like I might be kept by her for a few more years. There is no doubt, however, that our long-lasting marriage has had more to do with her wisdom and patience than my knowledge of women. To be honest, I still haven't figured her out completely. I guess it's because she keeps changing on me.

A FEW OBSERVATIONS

Coming from such a subservient position in our society, the advancements that women have made are phenomenal. From not being trusted with the vote and considered not capable of managing men, to becoming CEO's of Fortune 500 companies such as Xerox, IBM, and Walmart; Senators, Cabinet officials,

Supreme Court Justices, and now Vice President, there is no doubt about the progress women have made in our society. Why then, when women constitute fifty percent of our population, fifty percent of all college degrees, and forty-eight percent of our workforce, are there not that kind of representation in our organization's C-Suites?

The answer to that question I feel is two-fold. First and foremost are the traditional and antiquated views of men in power as to the capabilities of women and the role they should play in our system. Women have always played a subservient and supportive role in men's lives and many men cannot move past that image. It is slowly changing now but men growing up in traditional families always saw their mothers in that supportive role and saw that it was acceptable to mom. Then add the early channeling of young women into the occupations of teaching, nursing, and even homemaking, allowing men to believe that care-taking was clearly the role that women were good at and wanted.

THE CHALLENGE IS SYSTEMIC

The role that women should play in our society is not only in the minds of men but also is now baked into our system. It is still very much ingrained into the visions of many young girls today.

I mentioned earlier about the study that showed young girls who were very astute in math and science losing interest in those areas at the age of twelve or thirteen. It was an age where they started to realize that those areas of study were reserved for boys and that they should move on to other interests.

One of the accomplishments as Chairman that I am most proud was to help join the Girls Club with the Boys Club. I realize that there are some who believe that young girls need to be separated early in life to allow them to discover themselves without the outside influence of being around boys. I contend that the earlier the two cultures meet, the better. Although many chapters have combined the Boy's and Girl's Club in their communities, the two national organizations have not yet done so.

Both points have valid arguments but I feel the earlier we can get our young girls comfortable competing in the male-oriented culture, the better prepared they will be later in life to compete with men. The earlier they can learn that the male culture is not such a big deal, the better. I know when growing up and had Black and White YMCA's and Black and White scout troops, in my mind, it falsely made the white organizations seem better if not superior. It took some years for me to learn that was not the case but that could have been discovered by me early if allowed to associate with white children in their organizations. When young girls can associate and compete in the male culture at an early age, they become fluent in that culture and quickly realize that competing with men is well within their reach.

TRACKING SPORTS AND THE PROGRESS OF WOMEN

Everyone would agree that we are an intense sports-minded nation. This can be seen in the national interest that is displayed in events such as the World Series in baseball, the NBA playoffs, and the final four playoffs in college basketball. The Super Bowl is almost becoming a national holiday with most Americans watching the game at parties that are held all over our country. These parties and the game are enjoyed by men and women alike, which indicates we have come a long way in this area.

If we go back to the fifties, I can remember the introduction of women's basketball into high schools around the country. Being afraid that the sport was far too vigorous for young girls to play the game the same way boys did, they devised a game where any girl could only play on one half of the court at a time. To prevent exhaustion, no girl was allowed to run past mid-court.

Even as late as the eighties, I had to apologize to women in my training classes when I would use sports examples to make a business point because women thought such examples separated women from the business scenario because sports were for men. They felt that any reference to sports automatically was trying to eliminate women from the business conversation.

Then came Title IX, the civil rights legislation that prohibited sex-based discrimination in any school or education institution that received government funding. This legislation allowed young girls to enter the world of sports. We can now see when you let any group into a game, how quickly that group can become active participants in that game. Since the days of half-court basketball for girls, women have become an integral part of the American sports scene. In colleges today, young women can compete in sports that include basketball, softball, volleyball, swimming, diving, track and field and the list goes on. Even the sacred male stronghold of football was penetrated when Sarah Fuller scored the first point in college football by a woman. She played for Vanderbilt University and kicked a field goal in a game that made history.

Of course, now in professional sports, not only do we have women's basketball, tennis, and golf leagues but also there are professional women boxers, wrestlers, coaches on professional football and basketball teams, and referees in pro basketball and football. There was even a woman that made the officiating team of the 2021 Super Bowl.

It is fair to say that speakers no longer have to apologize when they use a sports example when referring to business situations. Of course, legislation was key in opening opportunities for women in sports, but also a major factor has been the change in women's attitudes that sports are exclusively a man's activity. Women have joined the once all-male arena and made themselves included in that world. Not only did we find out that women could understand the world of sports but also that they could participate very effectively in that world as well. This is a case of women not trying to change our nation from being so sports-minded (which will never happen) to change their mindset about sports and becoming part of that system. Women discovered that sports were not that complicated, nor that manly and by participating, they found out that they did not lose their femininity. With sports today, many women have left their "mental reservations" with regard to sports and have joined the American mainstream in this area.

GENDER, THE BIG MENTAL DIVISION

Without a doubt, one of the largest "reservations" in our system is the one relegated to women. Their reservation is not physical, for women have always lived with men, with a few exceptions such as an all-girls school or college. Women grow up with fathers and brothers and later in life live with boyfriends and husbands and work with male associates. They have plenty of opportunities to observe and adapt to the male culture. However, this adaptation has traditionally been from a second class or subservient position, not as equals. As mentioned, our society has always expected women to play a supportive role to the men with whom they associate.

Of course, this is slowly changing for women. I suggest slowly changing because, although a small percentage of men are moving away from this traditional view of women, the male culture still believes that this should be the case. Reversing this point of view for men is usually accomplished by individual women redefining their relationships with men, demanding more leadership roles in organizations, and taking their grievances to the Human Resources department when being treated unfairly. Today, it is harder for some men to assign a supportive role to their significant other when she makes more than he does and has greater potential for advancement. And so, "times, they are a changing" but ever so slowly. Just to get paid the same as a man for doing the identical job is still not within the grasp of the still dominant male culture.

BREAKING FREE FROM THE WOMEN'S MENTAL RESERVATION

So, if not relegated to be separated by men physically, and we see men beginning to accept women as equal competitors and even leaders more and more, why aren't women making greater progress? It could be that the women's culture is such a strong one that it has convinced many women they truly are not equal to men and cannot compete effectively with them. This, of course, has no place in reality and is true only if a woman believes it to be true. If a woman does believe it, then it will become a reality and will be the factor that defines her and will be key in defining her male relationships, both at home and at work. You can imagine if a young girl grows up seeing her mother playing a supportive role to her father and that her brothers helped Dad with the important tough work outside while she was relegated to washing dishes and cleaning the house are events that can have a telling effect on any woman's perspective later in her life.

Remember, we said that values you have at eighteen, are ones you carry for the rest of your life unless you make a deliberate attempt to change them. So, if that view of being a supportive person is to change, it must come from within every individual woman. In summary, if our society will not change fast enough for your life if the male culture is pretty much stuck in place and any given man is not open to changing their perspective, it looks like every woman must take it upon herself to force the change that must be made for her life.

Changing the attitudes of women who have accepted the "supportive only" role of men is not an easy task. During the fight for women's right to vote, although the majority of men were against it, major opposition came from women who thought that voting for women would upset the balance of nature and fought fiercely to stop women from gaining the vote. We also saw the same resistance from women when they were accepted into the various military branches.

Since that time, however, more and more women are leaving the "women's reservation" and moving to mainstream America in major contributing roles, although those advancements are impressive, I think we all know that they are just the tip of the iceberg as to the contributions women will make to our nation in the future.

GOLF ANYONE?

Golf is a fun activity but is also clearly a business tool. We often hear that many business deals are made on the golf course. This is not entirely true because business deals are rarely discussed while playing golf. What is true, however, golf allows individuals to get to know each other and start the building of relationships that could very well end in helping to make a business transaction. Spending five to six hours with a person in a relaxing environment bodes well for anyone who wants to make a connection and a round of golf has proven to be a successful vehicle for cementing relationships.

Women have often protested that golf should not be used this way because they feel they are cut out of this process. The claim is that golf is a man's game. Facts, however, do not bear this out. It was Mary Queen of Scots who commissioned the building of St. Andrews in the 1550s and was admonished by the Church of England because she was playing golf the day before her husband's funeral. In my office, I have a picture of women playing golf that is dated 1894 and it is reported that Queen Elizabeth 1 used her cadets to carry her golf clubs and coined the term caddy.

It is reported that women were some of the first to play golf in this country. One of the first private golf clubs established in the United States was in West Chester County, New York, and was for "Women Only." We also know that there isn't a golf course constructed anywhere in the world that doesn't have the facility for women to play from the "ladies' tees."

A final argument that golf is not merely a man's game is to watch the young women play golf on the LPGA tour. Those young women are the envy of at least nine-five percent of all male golfers. I, for one, can only wish I could play anywhere close to their ability. The challenge for women who do not play the game but are hesitant because of their gender is totally mental. Those who are hesitant must come off their reservation and realize that golf is a business tool available to everyone who wants to try it. If you decide to not play, don't worry about it. There are many successful male executives that don't play golf and it hasn't limited their careers. They just have found other avenues to help them make their connections.

A FINAL THOUGHT

If we can use golf symbolically and apply it to all things that are in the "unwritten rules" of our system that has their origin from the male culture, there are too many to list. Not all of these traditions will survive and others will be updated to match our changing America. But there will be other traditions like golf and sports that are not going away. But just as women have learned to understand, accept, and now become participants in golf and other sports and thus become part of the conversation in those areas, the same approach should be considered in other areas as well.

One of the great challenges for any woman is to not fear or even hesitate to step into once sacred areas of the male reservation. Whether it is being the one woman in the Saturday golf foursome or the only woman on your work team at the bar after work, this is a win/win for all. You will soon be seen as an equal with the group. You will learn what are the hot issues you should know and you will become more comfortable with the male culture. The men will get to know the real you and most importantly your presence will start to change the male culture to be more accepting of other women. If progress is to continue in the area of developing more women to take over leadership roles, it will take both men getting comfortable and accepting women in those leadership roles and women accepting the rules of the system and competing and winning under those rules.

Once a woman has obtained a leadership position, as the "unwritten rules" state: "Whoever is at the top of the pyramid has the right to make the rules." When at the top, if she can't change the rules completely, she at a minimum can alter the rules by making them more comfortable for other women who will follow. Just the fact that the boss is a woman automatically changes the once all-male culture in that business environment. It is slow, but progress is being made.

CHAPTER FOURTEEN

THE RULES OF MAINSTREAM AMERICA: *THE "UNWRITTEN RULES" OF THE GAME*

In a previous book entitled **"Empowering Yourself: The Organizational Game Revealed,"** I spell out in detail, what are the "unwritten rules" of our system, as well as the key skills one should learn if they are to succeed in what I call "the game." Here is a brief summary of those rules.

THE P.I.E. MODEL(c)

The success formula that I developed and again is only briefly described below, is called my **P.I.E MODEL** which stands for **P**erformance, **I**mage, and **E**xposure.

<u>PERFORMANCE</u>

The major revelation in the P.I.E. Model is that a person's performance will never have more than a **10%** impact on their upward mobility success no matter how good they are or how hard they work. It is the major reason why people hit "glass ceilings" as I did, in their careers. Most people think that when they become the best performer on their job, they deserve and are owed a promotion. The fact is, people are never promoted simply because they do their current job well. The only reward for a good performance in our system is a raise, bonus, or larger commission check. After that is paid, the organizational contract has been fulfilled. At this point, a person has been paid for their performance, and the organization owes nothing more to that worker. For students, the same holds true for grade point averages.

To apply to a premier college or get a job in a quality organization, whether it is an intern position or a permanent position after graduation, all competitive candidates will have a 3.8 to 4.0-grade point average and thus grades are nothing more than an entry requirement that allows you to enter the competition. At this point, the "unwritten rules" which I write about take over.

To understand "the game" we are currently playing in our society, as well as the global economy, we must go back 806 years to 1215 A.D. and the start of the British Empire. One of the major unwritten rules in the game is "Anyone at the top of any pyramid has the right to make the rules" (i.e., parents in a home, teachers in a classroom, generals in the army, or the Pope in the Catholic church). When it was said that the "sun never sets on the British Empire," England was on top of the then global economy or, in essence, the global pyramid. As a result, England had the right to make the rules for the system that currently exists. It is no accident that the world speaks English, and at the top of every society in the world, people play golf (St. Andrews), tennis (Wimbledon), the fact that she is an island, they sail and do activities on a horse (polo, fox hunting, horse racing). All of these activities emanated from the British Empire. China is an example that shows how the entire world has embraced these rules.

Since China has joined the global economy, they have built over five hundred golf courses and require every student at their top universities to take golf lessons before they can graduate. They also require every student from the third grade until they complete the rest of their formal education, to take a minimum of one English class every year. China will soon become the largest English-speaking nation in the world. They are preparing their children to be able to operate effectively at the highest levels of the global system and understand that the global system has very specific rules which I describe in my books. My first book has been translated into Chinese.

Shakespeare told us the world is a stage and that we are mere players. The player aspect is true but my research revealed that the world has seven stages or levels, each with its own lifestyle activities, value systems, and codes of conduct. These seven levels are scientifically verified as the seven societal levels that are defined in any socio-economic textbook.

IMAGE

Image accounts for **30%** of a person's success. It is so very important because, in order to move to the next higher socio-economic level, you must first become comfortable with that higher level's customs, traditions, values, and social activities. In comparison, if you want to work in France, no matter how technically efficient you are in your skill area, you must be able to speak French in order to be accepted, understood, and successful. The same is true if you have a job at level three in our system and want to compete for a position that is in level four. In order to be competitive, you must show that you can comfortably do the things that level four people will be doing. A simple example would be that you might have to trade in bowling for playing golf if you want a higher position. The simple reason is that your peers, clients, and the managers with whom you are required to interact at that higher level will not be found at the bowling alley. The "unwritten rule" that explains this situation is "You must look and act the part before you can be considered for that part" and/or "Don't dress (or more importantly conduct yourself) for the job you are in, but instead for the job you want." I have outlined below in detail the codes of conduct, values, and lifestyle activities that are required for each of the seven levels.

EXPOSURE

Exposure constitutes **60%** of a person's success. This is simply because the only way you can get to the next higher level is to have someone at that higher level pull you up to it. You can never be pushed up by employees or elected up by your peers. The person that pulls you from above is called a **sponsor**. In this game that we all play, if you want to advance to the next higher socio-economic level, you **must** have a sponsor. The difficult challenge is that a sponsor cannot support you and/or move you until they are sure you won't embarrass them by not being able to fit in at the level they want to promote you. As a result, they need to see you (preferably in social situations, especially for upper-level positions) to be assured that you have developed a comfort level in the lifestyle of the job for which you are being considered. To not fit into that upper-level of lifestyle, a person will usually be seen as a "token" and become ineffective in that position very quickly. It would be much like the Clampetts in "The Beverly Hillbillies" who called their swimming pool "the cement pond" and served possum for dinner.

PROOF THAT KNOWING AND PLAYING BY THE RULES REALLY WORKS

By learning and playing by the rules myself, I have tried to show it can have a powerful impact on a person's upward mobility. Starting from the working class and out of the mainstream life in which I began, playing by "the rules" has enabled me to be named "European Soldier of the Year" when stationed in Germany during the Berlin crisis. I became a board member of the Atlanta Girls Club for nine years. I chaired my final three years and helped lead the campaign to successfully combine the Boy's and Girl's Clubs. I have been elected to the Boards of, The National Girls Club, The Atlanta Boys Scouts, The Atlanta Neighborhood Justice Center, and Saint Joseph Hospital, selected to Leadership Atlanta, and was chosen the first "Small Businessman of the Year" by the Greater Atlanta Chamber of Commerce.

In addition, I was a consultant to England's House of Lords, a guest lecturer at MBA programs at such Universities as Wharton, Emory, Georgia Tech, Carnegie-Mellon, was an instructor at IBM's International Executive School in Brussels, GE's International Executive School and have been an executive coach to many Fortune 500 executives. Currently, I sit on the Board of Advisors of the Atlanta Ballet and the Georgia Museum of Art.

What this merely shows is anyone knowing the rules can make an impact on our society if only they learn how our system works and can gain knowledge of its "unwritten rules." This is the major reason I want to expose my information to the increasing number of women, minorities, and immigrants that are growing in numbers in our labor force today. However, I have found that even successful white executives, although they have played by the rules, were not conscious of the things they did to reach their current positions. They just were lucky to get into circles that practiced the mainstream rules and went along with the crowd.

BELOW ARE THE TWO "LIFESTYLE GAME CHARTS" THAT DESCRIBE THE SEVEN LEVELS OF OUR SYSTEM

LIFESTYLE ACTIVITIES

CATEGORIES	1	2	3	4	5	6	7
SOCIO-ECONOMIC CLASS TITLES	DROP-OUT CLASS	WELFARE, POVERTY CLASS	LABOR CLASS, LOWER-MIDDLE, BLUE COLLAR, WORKING CLASS	STANDARD-MIDDLE, SUBURBAN-MIDDLE, WHITE COLLAR, PROFESSIONAL, MANAGERIAL	HIGH LEVEL, UPPER MIDDLE CLASS	CELEBRITY, NOUVEAU RICHE, LOWER-UPPER, JET SET	ELITE, TOP UPPER -UPPER, ARISTOCRATIC, GOVERNING, OLD MONEY
EDUCATION	1-2 YEARS OF HIGH SCHOOL	POSSIBLY HIGH SCHOOL DEGREE	USUALLY HIGH SCHOOL DEGREE	COMMERCIAL ASSOCIATE DEGREE, TECHNICAL AND JUNIOR COLLEGE DEGREE	COLLEGE DEGREE, SOLID SCHOOLS	ADVANCED DEGREE, BETTER SCHOOLS	ADVANCED DEGREE, BEST SCHOOLS, BOARDING/PREP SCHOOLS
OCCUPATION	OUT OF WORK	PART-TIME WORKER AT MINIMUM WAGE	NON-EXEMPT MANUAL ADMINISTRATIVE WORKERS	EXEMPT, ACCOUNTANTS, PROGRAMMERS, SALES REPS, MANAGERS	MIDDLE MANAGEMENT, SMALL BUSINESS OWNER, AIRLINE PILOTS, MEDICAL, PROFESSIONALS	REGIONAL POLITICANS, TOP CORPORATE EXEC"S, MOVIE, TV, SPORTS PERSONALITIES	FAMILY BUSINESS, NATIONAL POLITICS, WALL STREET LAWYERS, TOP 20 BANKS
ORGANIZATIONS AND CLUBS	CHURCH CLUB	YM.C.A./Y.W.C.A. BOYS/GIRLS CLUBS, CHURCH RELATED CLUBS	MOOSE CLUB, EAGLE LODGE, CULTURAL CLUBS, GUN CLUBS	MASONS, ROTARY NON-PROFIT, CIVIC ORGANIZATIONS	NEIGHBORHOOD COUNTRY CLUBS, SWIM/TENNIS CLUBS	REGIONAL COUNTRY CLUBS, LOCAL COMMUNITY AND BOARDS	EXCLUSIVE NATIONAL SOCIAL CLUBS, PROFIT & NON-PROFIT NATIONAL BOARDS
SOCIAL ACTIVITIES	CHURCH RELATED	TV CHURCH	MOVIES, HUNTING, FISHING, CAMPING, FAMILY ACTIVITIES, BOWLING	ENTRY LEVEL, THEATER, TENNIS, GOLF	MORE ACCOMPLISHED IN SPORTS AND CULTURAL EVENTS, ENTRY LEVEL SKIING & BRIDGE	SAILING, SKIING, FLYING, CHARITY DRIVES	YACHTING, HORSE BREEDING, PATRON FINE ARTS, FOX HUNTING, POLO
LOCATION AND TYPE OF HOUSE	HOUSING PROJECTS, INNER CITY, HOMELESS	HOUSING PROJECTS, INNER CITY, RENT SUBSIDIZED	URBAN AREAS, OWN MOBILE HOME, ETHNIC COMMUNITIES	OWN HOMES IN SUBURBAN COMMUNITIES, TRACT HOUSES	COUNTRY CLUB COMMUNITIES, IN-TOWN RENOVATIONS	EXTRA LARGE HOMES, CUSTOM BUILT	MANSIONS, MULTIPLE HOMES

© Coleman Management Consultants, Inc.

LIFESTYLE ACTIVITIES

CATEGORIES	1	2	3	4	5	6	7
ENTERTAINING IN THE HOME	RARELY ENTERTAIN	EXTENDED FAMILY MEMBERS, HOLIDAYS	FAMILY & FRIENDS, BARBECUES, CASUAL	SOCIAL COCKTAIL PARTIES, SELF PREPARED, SPORTY	COCKTAIL PARTIES, BUSINESS & SOCIAL, CATERED, DRESSY	DINNER PARTIES BUSINESS & SOCIAL CATERED, DRESSY	DINNER PARTIES, VERY POLITICAL, EXTRAVAGANT FORMAL
EARNING POWER	NONE	$8,000-$35,000	$12,000-$75,000	$18,000-$250,000	$100,000-$500,000	$250,000 MILLIONS AND ABOVE	MILLIONS, INHERITED WEALTH
OTHER INVESTMENTS	NONE	NONE	SAVINGS SERIES "E" BONDS, LOTTERY TICKETS	INNER CITY CONDO, IRA'S, C.D.'S, TREASURY BONDS	VACATION HOME, INVESTMENT PORTFOLIO	LIMITED GENERAL PARTNERSHIPS, REVENUE PRODUCING PROPERTIES	STOCK OWNERSHIP, INTERLOCKING DIRECTORIES
FINE ARTS	NEVER ATTEND THEATER	RARELY ATTEND THEATER	ATTEND POPULAR THEATER PRODUCTIONS	MAINLY THEATER, SOME BALLET, OPERA, SYMPHONY, MUSEUM	SEASON TICKETS, BALLET, OPERA, SYMPHONY, MUSEUM	SERVE ON FINE ARTS COMMITTEES & BOARDS,	PATRON OF THE FINE ARTS
CAR	NO CAR	1 USED CAR	INTERMEDIATE SIZE, USED CAR, PICK UP TRUCK	BIG AMERICAN CAR, 1 OTHER USED CAR	MERCEDES, LEXUS, CADILLAC, OTHER LUXURY CARS	ROLLS ROYCE, BENTLEY, MULTIPLE CARS	CHAUFFEUR DRIVEN LIMOUSINE
VACATION ACTIVITIES	NONE	HOME TO PARENTS	1 WEEK FAMILY VACATION, HOME TO PARENTS	1 WEEK SHORE, MOUNTAINS, 1 WEEK HOME TO PARENTS	U.S.A. VACATION, CRUISES, SHORE, MOUNTAINS	EXCLUSIVE RESORTS ABROAD ONCE A YEAR	MOST EXCLUSIVE RESORTS, VACATIONS ABROAD, SEASONAL HOMES
COMMITTEES & BOARDS	NOT INVOLVED	INVOLVED IN CHURCH WORK	NON-PROFIT VOLUNTEER WORK IN ETHNIC COMMUNITIES	ON COMMITTEES OF MAINSTREAM NON-PROFIT ORGANIZATIONS	CHAIR COMMITTEES OF MAJOR NON-PROFIT ORGANIZATIONS	ON BOARDS, NON-PROFIT REGIONAL CORPORATIONS, LOCAL ARTS	CHAIR BOARDS OF NATIONAL NON-PROFIT MAJOR CORPS., FINE ARTS

© Coleman Management Consultants, Inc.

Another book I have written is entitled, **"Rules of the Game for High School, College and Life."** Two of the most frequent comments I hear from older individuals are, "Why didn't someone tell me about these rules 20/30 years ago?" And "How do I get this information to my children?" My research uncovered that the "game" in all of our lives, starts in the seventh grade. From K-6, we expect our children to learn by rote such things as their timetables and the alphabet. It's in the seventh grade that we give children the freedom to choose their extracurricular activities that could impact them for the rest of their lives.

Those choices could include playing on the basketball team or the golf team, the football team, or the tennis team. Do they want to play an instrument in the school orchestra, run for student council or be in the annual school play? They may seem like insignificant choices for many minority students and when made, could often separate them from their racial or cultural peers.

However, many of those activities are preparing a child for the upper-level positions for which they will compete later in their life and career. Boarding and private schools do not give children those choices because they are built into their core curriculum. Even those children who do not go out for the golf and tennis teams in their schools are exposed to those activities at their parents' country clubs. Upper-level parents understand (like in China which requires golf lessons to graduate from their top Universities) that these activities are preparing their children to one day be effective at the top levels of the global system. I also have written a discussion guide for teachers, parents, and youth leaders to help young adults sort through the many decisions they must make during their early high school years.

CHAPTER FIFTEEN

THE POSITIVES AND NEGATIVES OF PLAYING THE GAME

MY PERSONAL CHANGE AND MOVING ON

As mentioned before, I grew up in a working-class family and environment. As a result, in my youth, it required me to work many service jobs in social environments where the game was being played. To chart my journey to mainstream America, I started out in a street gang but later became an Eagle Scout. With sports, I began by playing football, baseball, basketball, and running track. Eventually in my life, I moved from those activities to playing golf, tennis, sailing, skiing, playing bridge, and chess. In music, I started with my Doo-wop singing group.

However, later, I became a member of Wilberforce University's concert traveling choir, a singer in two folk groups, and a member of a barbershop quartet. I have attended over three hundred Broadway musicals (a hobby) and have held season tickets with the Atlanta Symphony, Ballet, and Opera companies for several years. This is to say that my interests were in a constant state of change and now that I look back, I was very fortunate to have tried so many things. It provided me with a lot of fun, helped me to grow as a person, and gave me the opportunity to meet a lot of interesting and knowledgeable people.

Much of the knowledge I gained of the rules came from my work experiences. Although I made some mistakes with many of my decisions, those wrong decisions gave me valuable input on what not to do in future similar situations when they occurred. It is true about the sayings, "That what doesn't kill you will only make you stronger" and "Where there's no pain, there is usually no gain."

From a corporate work perspective, Xerox Corporation hired me as its first Black salesman in the nation, a few months after the Civil Rights Act was passed in 1964. Three years later, I joined the IBM Corporation for twelve years working in sales, Equal Employment Opportunity, and management training and left them as a Divisional Headquarters Human Resources Manager. It is the experience I had in hitting a "glass ceiling" at IBM, that allowed me to gain the knowledge and perspective that I offer in my books and teach in my classes.

In 1980, I started my own firm, Coleman Management Consultants, Inc., training executives, Women, and Minority Employee Groups, by speaking at MBA programs and at conventions. I was teaching what I had learned about Diversity issues in our country, as well as sharing the "unwritten rules" of our system and how it works.

When I first started, I was speaking to Black groups during one of our country's rioting periods and with female groups during the seventies women's revolution. Many thought I was selling out to the "white man" when I shared my information. It was viewed that I was supporting their organization's platform instead of their concerns. At the time, my staff warned me that I could be physically harmed by radical members of those groups or by the establishment who didn't want anyone outside of their circle of power to learn the rules. I remember people in the audience often shouting out that I was an "Uncle Tom" or a "Chauvinist" when I was speaking.

I vividly remember once walking into a seminar of Black participants in Liberty City, Florida two weeks after the riots that occurred there in 1980. The entire back row had their chairs turned around with their backs facing me. They said after we began to dialogue that they didn't want to listen to the white man's messages that I was being paid to deliver. By the end of the three days that we had together, we were able to work things out. That became possible when they discovered that there were rules by which they could play that would make a difference in their career advancement. It gave them a sense of control and allowed them to feel that they were just victims of our system.

Unfortunately, in my current training sessions, I'm still running into attitudes of young Black employees and managers that think playing by mainstream America's rules is selling out. My response to those individuals is that they should consider coming off their "mental reservations" where they might have placed themselves if they want to make a greater impact in our total society.

LEAVING PEOPLE BEHIND

One of the most stressful experiences of joining mainstream America is the awful and sometimes guilty feeling one gets when one must leave people behind. If you want an upward-oriented career, this is something you must do. It doesn't make it any easier but it is something most of us have done all of our lives. If you don't think you have ever experienced this, I ask that you go back to your old neighborhood and meet with some of your best friends from high school that still live in the old neighborhood. The first night that you meet with them, you have one of your greatest evenings. You stay up until three in the morning recalling all of your great experiences in high school. It's an evening of "remember that time when."

The second night you meet, since all the old times have been covered, you begin talking about your current life. It could include sharing the fact that you are a second-level manager, that you just bought a new home or a small fishing boat, and other of your current life's activities. But as you look up and your old friends are just staring at you, you realize that they think you are bragging. Not wanting to be viewed as a braggart, you stop talking about your life. As they talk about their lives you quickly conclude that very little has changed in the neighborhood in the last twenty years. On the third night, you are supposed to meet, but you find an excuse as to why you can't.

All of these dynamics suggest that you are just experiencing the "unwritten rule" that tells us, "You can't go home again." Oh, you can go home to visit, always to help out when needed, to ensure that you stay in touch, or just to go back to let everyone know you still love them. But you can't stay very long. After you make sure everyone is fine and you accomplish the chores that mom and dad want you to do, you end up watching soap operas and quickly conclude that it is time to go back to the world in which you currently live. You have learned a new language and now live in another world in which you find comfortable and challenging. Although you might feel guilty, it is no one's fault. You have changed and they have not. That is a fact of life that will never change.

I tell people that if they would take me to their family reunion, by three o'clock I will be able to point out every working-class cousin and every professional cousin in your family. It is because, by that time, they are all in separate groups. The morning is spent reconnecting with everyone to catch up but once that is done, cousins need to be comfortable with any further conversations. Even family blood cannot overcome this rule.

The rule becomes more significant in the relationship with your "significant other." If one partner moves to the next higher socio-economic level and does not mentor and/or sponsor their mate to join them, that relationship is in serious danger of breaking up. They will soon be living in two different worlds and we know about the fate of "a house divided." This becomes more pronounced the higher the level that one of the partners chooses to go. When it is important to combine your work requirements with your social life such as client cocktail parties, community organization banquets, and artistic events; having your partner be there and supportive is a necessity. If they do not adapt to that higher level and the relationship falls apart, we just say "They just grew apart." Even our personal relationships are not above this rule.

This is why those who want upward-oriented careers should really be thinking of life planning, not just career planning. At certain levels in our system, our careers and social lives collide and become very much intermingled. This often requires leaving people behind and again, it is one of the most emotional and difficult aspects but a requirement of the game.

Playing by mainstream rules can be very troubling to any individual that is surrounded by individuals who look at the world from a tribal perspective. In these environments, you must be prepared to take a lot of spears and arrows that will challenge your loyalty to the culture and even your wisdom in trying to move on. It is one of the reasons this book is entitled, "The Difficult and Challenging Journey to Mainstream America" because the road can be rocky indeed. Much of that difficulty might come from both family and friends who might be discouraging you to not change from the person they know and love. In their subconscious, they know that the changes they see you making are the beginning of a separation that will happen if they choose not to go with you. It's normal, it's natural but difficult. "Letting go" of old relationships is always hard. It's not like you're dying, but slowly the relationships you had with many friends will slowly fade from their former intensity because you are moving on. Since most of us have done it before and if you want an upwardly mobile career you may have to do it several more times before you reach your personal career objectives. Of course, you should at least try to stay as connected to old relationships that time will allow but the fading of those old ties doesn't get any easier emotionally. Just relish the fact that you will always meet new people who will fill the void.

Not everyone will, nor should, leave their physical and/or mental reservations or communities of comfort. Great contributions can and need to be made within all of them. However, as individuals, we have the freedom to make the choice to stay or leave. I have witnessed many deciding to leave, once they have an understanding of the rules.

CHAPTER SIXTEEN

MAKING THE BUSINESS CASE FOR TEACHING THE RULES

One of those "unwritten rules" in our system is "Never present a problem without also offering a solution." If that is the case, I have clearly presented a challenge for our nation, our organizations, and for every individual. Let me not violate that rule and suggest some solutions that each of those entities might consider.

THE BUSINESS CASE FOR TEACHING THE RULES FOR ORGANIZATIONS

Red vs Blue

The divisions in our society is obvious. These divisions can be labeled in terms of Red vs Blue States, Democratic vs Republican vs Progressive parties, or Liberal vs Conservative political philosophies. As the French would say, "vive la difference." In a democracy, we understand that there will always be differences of opinion within the population. However, in today's political climate, these differences have reached extremely high emotional levels and have been strong enough to sever relationships not only between friends but also among family members as well.

After the 2020 presidential race that we have just endured, many historians have stated that we have not been this divided as a nation since the Civil War. I think we all know that if we want to remain competitive as a nation in the global economy, we must repair our divisions and start to work together if we are to succeed in the future. As Abraham Lincoln stated, "A house divided against itself cannot stand." The skills that we must now rely on are those of effective communication, meaningful dialogue, compromise, understanding, empathy and to reach the sharing of common values. We are not alone in this challenge as a nation. With the migration of the world population and the massive immigration that is being experienced in many countries, cultural conflicts are becoming a major issue in many societies.

The challenge in our country is even greater than most because our political differences do not have notable lines of separation as the Mason/Dixon Line did before the Civil War. People who might disagree with your political philosophy may live next door, attend the same religious institution, are parents on your child's sports team, or even work beside you on your job. We would like to think that we all can leave our emotional feelings at home and not let them interfere with our relationships in our other environments, but that is difficult for many and impossible for some. When emotional differences are brought into the workplace, it can have a tremendous impact on team relationships and eventually the success of the organization's mission. All it might take is one person stating a political position, and three teammates might make the decision to not share important information with that person or at a minimum start to socially isolate them.

AN ORGANIZATIONAL SOLUTION

This is a situation that organizations cannot let go unchecked. If they are going to try to maximize productivity on work teams, they must create environments where associates can seek common values and develop a common language in which they can exchange ideas and work information. This is where knowledge of the "unwritten rules" on how our organizational system works become of paramount importance. Think of it in sports terms. If you were a coach of a basketball team and wanted to win a championship, would you only share the rules of that game with a few of your players or brief half of the team on the game plan you had for the next important game? Of course not. Anyone would consider that a failing strategy. How could a team mold itself into a championship team with only a few members knowing the rules? The main purpose of the coaching staff is to not only ensure that every player knows the rules but to work on every individual's weaknesses making them the best possible player they can be. Anything short of that would be a major flaw in that coaching staff.

The same scenario applies to our work environments. With the many cultures, life experiences, perspectives, political positions, and values that now represent our work teams, to not give them a common vehicle that would allow everyone to come together in a common place with a common language and a common set of rules would be extremely destructive. This would apply not only to individuals and their personal growth but also to the team as a whole. Effective teams find ways for team members to connect with each other, and a common set of rules is a powerful method of doing this in the work environment. At a minimum, it levels the playing field giving everyone an equal chance to play and succeed under the same rules.

THE BENEFITS OF SHARING THE RULES WITH ALL

In addition to the win/win of higher motivational levels and attitudes of employees by sharing the rules, an increase in productivity and devotion to the mission of the organization is also gained. Sharing the rules with everyone will also:

- Assist in preventing the polarization of employees
- Open common lines of communication between managers/employees and among associates
- Give managers new agendas and information to help employees grow personally
- Allow participants to better understand the "trade-offs" they must consider for their future career advancement
- Help participants work through any cultural conflicts they may have with the organization's cultural rules
- Increase the leadership skills of all employees
- Provide a common set of values that can unite all individuals in the organization
- Can help a person clarify career objectives

- Level the playing field for all employees and create a healthy competitive working environment. It is true what President Ronald Reagan once told us, "Without competition, you cannot have excellence."

Of course, many executives today can justify their level of awareness because they have attended diversity or awareness training. But as we have mentioned before, diversity training for executives today usually comes in a two-hour executive overview which compares to someone wanting to learn French taking one lesson and expecting to be fluent upon completion of that lesson. In today's increasingly divided racial society, sharing the rules may well become even more difficult. An example might be as simple as telling a woman that she should take up golf like all the other male executives in the organization have done.

THE NEED TO LEARN THE RULES IN AN INCREASING GLOBAL ECONOMY

As organizations become more global, we can no longer send our employees into that diverse environment who can only translate the business message through their more personal and narrow cultural lenses. For us to do so would put them at an extreme disadvantage in presenting their ideas and messages to business people outside of our country. These challenges have already been accepted and solutions enacted by most other countries. The global business world now, for the most part, speaks English. For the most part, we do not see international business people showing up at meetings in Kilts, lederhosen, dashikis, or Kimonos. All may be colorful but by doing so, could possibly call into question that person's understanding and savvy of the current business norms.

We, as a country, will not be an exception to this rule. Other countries have made great efforts to instruct their business populations in the international language of business. Many years ago when I was instructing Japanese executives who were preparing to work in the United States, they would have the participants line up ten minutes before the class in two lines and practice shaking hands to get out of the habit of bowing. Initially, they would do both, but eventually, the bowing would subside as they got comfortable shaking hands. It was difficult for the

Japanese to rewrite their "gut level tape recorders" away from their familiar bowing tradition but they felt it was necessary to be more effective with business people outside of their culture. They understood that if you want to play any game successfully, you must play by the rules of that game. This is a lesson I feel that, as a country and as organizations, we are not teaching our young business people. It will put our future business representatives at a tremendous disadvantage when they must compete on a global level. Of course, the same dynamics apply domestically when our young diverse population wants to advance to higher levels and has not been taught the rules of those higher levels. We are doing them a great injustice by not sharing the requirements needed to reach and then succeed at higher levels.

This is not being done on purpose. There is no master plan to keep our young future leaders ignorant of the information that would allow them to reach their potential. Instead, it is being done to allow people of color and women to be comfortable in the workplace. We have defined a successful inclusion strategy as, denying that our system has rules, don't share how the system works, and thus making all diverse employees feel comfortable. The results of doing this have been costly in the form of people hitting glass ceilings without knowing why. This in turn heightens the frustration of feeling like they are "victims of the system." Finally, this leads to higher turnover, lower morale, and a reduction in loyalty to the organization. By continuing with this strategy, we can see that ultimately it will have a negative impact on the organization's mission or bottom line.

HOW CAN INDIVIDUALS LEARN THE RULES?

It has been stated often, you can't play any game effectively if you don't know the rules of that game. We have also made the case that these organizational rules that govern our career progression are often ones that are unwritten. As a result, you can't go to written resources like employee/management manuals or performance plans to get a sense of direction when lost or confused. The two major sources for this information are to read your environment and to find mentors and sponsors that can help you along your journey.

READING YOUR ENVIRONMENT

One of the more important skills that a game player needs to constantly sharpen is their ability to read the unwritten rules of the organization to which they belong. I discuss this skill in great detail in my first book: "Empowering Yourself: The Organizational Game Revealed, The Best Kept Secret in Organizational America." But with discussing our journey to mainstream America, it is important to quickly review the basic principles of reading one's environment.

Remember, a basic rule is that all rules flow in an organization from top to bottom. This tells us you should always look to your boss if you want to know the rules that affect you on a daily basis. You can usually count on him or her to display the rules that they wish their team to follow. Professionals generally agree on the importance of reading and then adapting to their environments. It is called survival. Those who do not accurately read and adapt to their environments usually come across as crude, uninformed, and lacking savvy–three bullets that can mortally wound any career.

Knowing the steps that are required to read the dynamics of any environment is critical. They include: observe, question, and interpret. If this is done effectively, a person is then in the position to make an accurate evaluation if they want to adapt to their environment's requirements. It is the decision to either adapt or not that will determine a person's success in their organization. Let's take a close look at each of those elements.

- **OBSERVE**: When you first arrive at a new location, it is important to be a silent observer. Take time to see who are the power players in the department and the organization. Who are the people that are listened to and who make the decisions on important issues? Observe what are the strategies of people who are advancing and who are the ones that have the ear of the management and executive team. If you can figure out how they have accomplished their success, you have a good foundation regarding some of the things you might want to consider.

- **QUESTION**: There will always be some things that might not be clear and obvious in your observations. Don't make wild guesses as to what is happening. As soon as possible, establish connections with some veteran employees. You can bring situations to them and get more detailed information. These mentoring relationships can usually be established by just asking a question. Most people are always willing to help and feel important when they can show their understanding of the dynamics of the organization. I have also found that once a person gives another individual advice, they are bound to stay connected to see if their advice was helpful. This can lead to a solid mentoring relationship that can, for many, last an entire career.

- **INTERPRET:** This next step is placed entirely on your shoulders. After you have collected all available information, it must be dissected, analyzed, evaluated, and given the most accurate interpretation possible, using all of your people and organizational experience. This is the information that will allow you to clarify all of your options to determine the choices you will eventually make. This is when and how you can determine for yourself if it is worth conforming to the unwritten requirements of the organization or not.

The most important skill during this period of information gathering is to listen. Important information is often passed on from mentors and/or sponsors that may be coded or put into the form of a sarcastic comment or even a joke. If a potential sponsor tells you something they suggest that you should consider in joking terms, they are not kidding. What they may be suggesting is their willingness to be a sponsor if you address the issue about which they have relayed to you in a joking manner. This may be a comment on your dress, your hairstyle, or even additional education you should consider. To refuse this advice might tell that potential sponsor that their sponsorship is not worth any further effort on their part because you are not willing to pay the dues they are suggesting. For example, if you respond to a joking comment about getting your hair cut differently with, "Oh, this is how my husband likes it" might just tell that potential sponsor, "I don't want your sponsorship if that is what I have to do."

Our nation, our organizations, and we ourselves are in a constant state of change. However, changes in organizations and our nation come at an alarmingly slow rate. Changes in our nation may take hundreds of years as witnessed by such issues as school desegregation, voting rights, and police brutality. Yes, things are getting better in all of those areas but it is a very slow process. Change in organizations happens a little faster, but in these environments, meaningful change can take many decades. This can be seen in the advancement of women and people of color to executive positions or even the length of time that it takes to make a factory environment safe. It will happen but it is not an overnight process.

The only way any person can expect to enjoy major career advancement in their lifetime is the degree to which they are willing to change themselves. Their own ability to adapt to the requirements of upper-level positions as an individual is totally in their hands and that time frame will be according to their motivational level. To sit and wait for the system to change to meet your values and your comfort zones is something that will, more than likely, not happen in your career time frame.

In relation to personal change, we once more have to go back to our old friend Will Rogers who reminds us: "In this game of life, when you are through changing, you are through."

CHAPTER SEVENTEEN

DECIDING IF THE JOURNEY IS RIGHT FOR YOU

CHOOSING THE LEVEL ON THE GAME BOARD YOU WOULD LIKE TO PLAY

This brings us to one of the most important questions that must be answered. Where do I want to play out my life in this game of life? Should I live my life staying in the world of my race, ethnic background, gender, and sexual orientation or should I live out my life in mainstream America? It is such a personal question; I can be of little help to anyone. The fact is, there is no right or wrong, good or bad answer to that question. Either choice has its advantages and its rewards. Which one is right for you is totally up to you. Again, I would advise you to make the choice that will make you happy.

One word of caution, happiness can be measured in the short term or long range. Short-term happiness can be often obtained by being comfortable in familiar environments and with people you are comfortable being around. It might also be found with work you love doing and the activities in which you are engaged and can do very well. You might ask, what's wrong with that? The answer is nothing. You see, you are the only critic of the choices you make. Of course, there will be many people who will give you well-intentioned advice as to what you should do with your life, but only you have to live with the results of your life choices.

If you are happy with the consequences of your choices after they are made, then it was the right choice for you. But we must remember that short-term happiness can fade very quickly as we grow through later life experiences. One should always think strategically. That is to say, "Will you be happy with your current contentment ten years from today?" "Will you still be happy with your current life situation in the future"? That can, of course, be very possible but not preparing for a future world can be very risky. One can easily wake up ten years in the future wishing they might have tried a few more new things, learned more about other subjects, or planned a little more carefully for the life that was to come. Life can be full of Monday morning quarterbacking with numerous statements of "I wish I would have... ." I have mentioned before that strategic thinking is one of the most difficult skills to master but clearly one of the most crucial.

This is a chapter that is difficult to write and remain totally neutral because it is full of opinions and in this case, they just happen to be mine. Like everyone, I can only evaluate life via my life experiences and through my own personal lenses. I have been fortunate to live on the Black reservation, the White suburban reservation, and mainstream America. I can honestly say that I wouldn't trade a moment of any one of them. Maybe it would be productive to examine the benefits of all three worlds.

THE CASE FOR STAYING ON CULTURAL RESERVATIONS

Your culture helps to define who you are

Living on a cultural reservation can be, as I experienced it, pure joy. It allows you to connect and feel a part of something special. They will be the most cherished memories that I will recall for the rest of my life. This is, I'm sure, the same with most people of all cultures. The sense of sharing a common history and common struggles creates a bond that cannot be matched with the exception of one's immediate family. By the way, your family is one of the major vehicles through which we are taught about our cultures. To not love your culture would be to a great extent saying you don't love your family. I would say that our family and the culture in which we grew up become the very foundation of who we are. At a minimum, it is from where it all began for all of us. It is in this environment many people create bonds that can last a lifetime. Is it any wonder that it's so difficult for anyone to leave their culture?

This was the case with me and my early black cultural experience but again, I'm sure difficulty in breaking from your roots is true with everyone coming from strong ethnic, racial and religious cultural reservations. Even the sub-cultures within these reservations, such as gender, age, and socio-economic levels, can create special bonds with group members that could last for the rest of your life.

THE PRIDE OF BELONGING

Another wonderful experience is the pride that one receives when members of their culture become successful and make contributions that benefit the mainstream population as well as their own. "Giving back" to one's culture is a way of making yourself a part of the history and progress of your people. To make contributions to one's culture is very much like giving to your immediate family. The pride and enriched feeling of doing this is a feeling that is rarely duplicated in one's life.

A large part of cultural pride is associated with that culture's foods and art forms. From an artistic perspective, living in a cultural reservation allows a person to study former contributions and then build upon them by raising, whatever that art form may be, to levels never seen before. As an example, this can be witnessed in the African-American culture in the area of music. From slave songs to gospel, blues, jazz, doo-wop, disco, and rap, all were creative art forms that made their way to mainstream America and added to the enjoyment of all music-loving Americans. Of course, not all cultural music gets to mainstream America, but usually, the best will break through. This process is often referred to as "cross-over."

This is of course true with music from every culture, whether it is the influence of a country and western song, Austrian waltz, a Polish polka, or songs from Mexico, the Caribbean Islands, or Ireland. When it reaches our mainstream, it adds to the richness of the continuous development of American music. Without the continual contributions that come from our many cultures in all artistic areas of life, we would not be the strong, creative, innovative, and influential country that we are. Remaining on a cultural reservation will allow you to continue with those creative contributions. The richness of mainstream America relies on the richness that comes from all of our cultural reservations.

A DESIRE TO HELP IMPROVE THE LIVES OF OTHERS

This does not apply to every cultural reservation but to such cultures as the Indigenous, Black, and Hispanic reservations, there is much that needs to be done to improve the lives of people within their geographic borders. The fight in these communities for equal justice, fair treatment by the police, access to financing, available and reasonable housing, better schools, and medical care are just a few of the issues that cannot be abandoned and need future leaders to continue the fight to level the playing field for their communities. Many professionals in the areas of medicine, education, and social work deliberately make the decision to practice their skills on their cultural reservations even at the expense of lower financial gains.

THE NEED TO SAVE AND PASS THE TRADITIONS ONTO FUTURE GENERATIONS

It is natural to want to save and preserve things that are beautiful. I do it all the time and save things that I would want to be passed down to my children if they want them. This is true with culture as well. The traditions we have that were passed along to us and are still practiced, are the things that hold families together. These can be religious observations, how we celebrate various holidays, and even the dishes that have been in the family for generations. All of these have a warming and bonding effect on all of us. Of course, just by doing these things, we have already passed those traditions on to our children. They then will do the same with their children. With the passing of each generation, there will always, however, be adjustments and modifications to those traditions to make them fit into their current environments. There might be times when your traditions may be altered by your children when they marry someone from another culture that brings with them their beloved traditions. This is when compromise happens and both cultural traditions are slightly changed. This combining of cultures is the melting pot in action. Out of that compromise for that family will come a new set of traditions. This process will continue and each time it happens, mainstream America is being formed and defined. This is something that cannot be stopped.

This is best illustrated when we look at languages. Many immigrants that came to our country wanted to preserve their native language via their children but soon lost hope in that happening the moment their children came into contact with mainstream children in school. To hope that they pay attention to their native language when their child realizes that English was the language needed for their survival in school and social life is a losing battle. I have talked to so many people who said they wished they would have learned the native language of their parents but didn't. The point is, they were too busy melting.

I am not suggesting that every culture should not try to instill their culture into their children, but the reality is children must live in a world that is current, not one of the past. The best we can do is pass on the values of our cultures to our children and let them take those values into the American mainstream. The strongest values of all of our cultures will survive in some form to make a better and stronger mainstream, and that is something of which any culture can be proud. With the personal social media vehicles available to young people today, they will define their culture according to the needs and wishes of their peers. Even authoritative countries are finding it harder to keep their people in line because the world, in its reality, is penetrating through their walls of enclosure because of modern media technology. For the good or bad of it, when truth and reality are learned, change is bound to happen.

MY EARLY MULTI-CULTURAL EXPERIENCES

The first phase of my life as I have shared was spent living in two worlds. I was on a physical reservation, living in a predominantly Italian community but socially lived in the "colored" community. Although as a child I had white childhood friends. My major social interactions were with my black friends across town revolving around my family's church, my Boy Scout troop, and my involvement with sports. My hometown was small enough to have only one high school. Therefore, I had the learning experience of living in two worlds. My freshman year of college was spent at Wilberforce University (a Historical Black University) and later transferred to Penn State University. I intensified my multi-cultural experience by joining the U.S. Army for three years and was stationed in Germany.

As I have explained before, from a gender perspective, I was a househusband for two years, and for three years was the only male employee among thirty-two women at Boyle-Kirkman Associates, the first women's consulting firm in the country.

With all my interactions with the Black, White, Italian, German, and Women's culture allowed me to grow comfortable with not only my native Black culture but also to see the richness that exists in people of all backgrounds. This was the foundation that allowed me to reach out to mainstream America later in my life.

CAN I LIVE IN MORE THAN ONE WORLD?

An answer to that question is easy. Of course, you can and many people do. We go back to the same point that there are neither right nor wrong choices as long as you are willing to accept the consequences of your choices. The bonus of living on both your cultural reservation as well as participating in the mainstream will broaden your life experiences. You have a chance to meet more people and personally be involved in both of those different environments.

The downside happens if you want to be considered a candidate for senior-level mainstream positions. If this is the case, you have chosen to compete for mainstream rewards along with many other candidates who will be vying for the same positions. It is fair to say that in these situations, it is "game on." Like any competitive situation, the winner is usually determined by a combination of skill, determination, and the amount of time and effort that the competitor is willing to dedicate to gain that position. Logic tells us if one of the competitors is willing to spend ninety percent of their time in the mainstream, competing for a mainstream job, and ten percent of their time on their reservation, and the other competitor chooses to split their time fifty/fifty between the two; in most competitive situations the most dedicated competitor that plays in the mainstream will usually win. In most competitive games we would usually think that is a fair way of determining the winner with the exception of promotions. For some reason, many think that this natural law should not apply to careers and upward mobility. An understanding of the rules tells us that the work environment is not an exception to this competitive dynamic. The statement, "Judge me by my performance" just doesn't hold water in the upward-oriented organizational game.

Whatever time you decide you want to spend learning and participating in the mainstream world, you will never completely disconnect from your racial or cultural roots. It is the core of who you are and you will always come back to it whenever you need a refill on love, memories, and old traditions and comforts. It is very much like family; you know to achieve your life goals might require that you leave them but you can't wait to get back home for the holidays. The same "letting go" is required if you want to be a serious contender for senior positions in an organization.

A REVIEW OF THE AFRICAN-AMERICAN JOURNEY

What I am about to say applies to all individuals of all races and cultures, but again may I take a moment to share a thought through my African-American lens? To members of my community, we do have the choice to remain on our reservation or choose to join mainstream America. That is an individual freedom for which many have fought and for which many have died. Will it be easy to play in the mainstream? Of course not! But for African-Americans, not attacking difficult problems has never been a consideration. As a community, it has never been easy, but that has never prevented us from taking on challenges that would allow us to move forward. Of course, this is something that all cultures can say about their history and journey as well. I guess it's just the American way.

THE LONELINESS OF BEING "THE ONLY"

As more people of color start to play the mainstream game and advance higher in the system, they won't have to experience the feeling of being alone. Until then, be prepared to enter many situations where you will often, from a cultural perspective, be the only one in your group present. If this happens, you are probably not at a mainstream event but more than likely are in a white reservation environment. One sweep of the room will allow you to make that determination. Do this merely, however, for your curiosity. There is no different action necessary on your part. When you find yourself in that situation often enough, you soon become so comfortable that you do not even think about it. That is a sign that you are becoming fluent and thus comfortable being on the "white reservation." Just relax and have fun.

When you are in a mainstream environment, however, you will usually not have to seek out people who look like you. They should be represented in the room. If not, there should be at least other people of color to indicate it may be a mainstream event. In this environment, you will not feel spotlighted, and you can be fairly assured that everyone in the room will be judged, "by the content of their character" and not by their cultural identification. When we can, as a society, get to where these multi-cultural, mainstream environments become commonplace, we will be moving closer to the dream that Dr. King envisioned.

We, of course, are a long way from being there, but I have personally witnessed our advancement in this area. Even though I can still remember the first "the talk" given to me by my father to not look white men directly in their eyes when I passed them on the street and the crosses that were burned on my three different lawns; I can honestly say today, "some of my best friends are white guys." Of course, our society has made progress but it has taken eighty years for me to personally experience this progress. I'm afraid it will take many more generations and the decision of many more individuals to join the American mainstream, from both the white and black reservations, before those "American melting pot" environments will happen in any great numbers.

The great thing about living in a democracy is that it gives everyone the freedom to chart their own destiny. This is done by the choices we make. Our future, both as individuals and as a nation, is in our own hands and will be predicated on what we want it to be. The choices that we are making today will define our future in both areas. As a nation, we have always boasted that our country is a melting pot and the choices we have made as a nation in the last sixty years have, for the most part, supported that goal. With the monumental choices that we have made such as the Constitutional changes giving women the right to vote, passing legislation such as the Civil Rights and Voting Rights Acts, and Supreme Court decisions such as Brown vs Kansas Board of Education which integrated our schools, have all moved us closer to tapping into all of the talents we have in our country. These measures have also moved more Americans into our mainstream. When I refer to more people who have joined the mainstream, I am referring to those people who were on their White, Black, Hispanic, Asian, religious, sexual orientation, and all the other mental reservations on which so many people live.

THE SLOW PROCESS OF AMERICA'S MELTING POT

We have seen by our history how long it takes for a new immigrant community to get a substantial amount of its people to leave their various communities and have that newly released talent starts to enrich our mainstream. We can chart this time frame by looking at past ethnic groups and their mainstream advancement such as the Irish and Italians.

The Irish for example came to America in great numbers because of the great potato famine during the 1850s. As with most immigrants that enter our country in large numbers, they located themselves on their community reservations. Their acceptance in the mainstream at that time was far from welcoming. White Anglo-Saxon Protestant or WASP was the major criteria of acceptance by the establishment at the time. The Irish were considered by that group to be the lowest of the low. Articles in the major newspapers in New York often referred to them as being subhuman. This is where they began their journey to mainstream America. It took approximately one hundred years (1860 to 1961) before we were comfortable enough to elect an Irish Catholic to the office of President. That would be a journey of five generations.

The Italian immigrant story is much the same. From their "Little Italy" beginnings, it took the same number of generations before an Italian woman (Nancy Pelosi) gain the position of Speaker of the House. Several Italian Americans have run for the office of

President but have not yet succeeded. What this tells us is that getting people to leave their racial and ethnic communities and getting our nation to accept their talents and contributions takes a long time.

By shutting out racial and ethnic groups from freely participating in our system, historically has forced some members of those communities to resort to illegal and criminal activities to survive. It is only after our society begins to level the playing field for that community and give them opportunities to play the mainstream game, do we see the next generation start to play by the rules of our system. Historically, criminal gangs that formed on the Irish, Italian, Black, Asian, Hispanic, and Jewish reservations have all been started by young people who felt that they were not allowed or did not know how to play in the American mainstream. That was true on the Irish, Italian and Jewish reservations in the twenties and thirties and is currently true in the Black and Hispanic reservations today. Once you give any community the opportunity and knowledge of how to compete in our system, we have seen a reduction in crime and an increase in the contributions they will make to our nation.

We can no longer wait for five generations to tap into our current young talented people of color and immigrant population. Our global competitors are not just standing by while we slowly develop our future talent. If we still want to maintain our place at the top of the global economy, we must start to recognize the critical need to give this important issue our full attention. Remember, by 2060, white males will constitute only twenty-nine percent of our nation's workforce. Those few numbers cannot carry seventy percent of our country on their backs alone. If we do not get more aggressive growing potential leaders in our entire population, we will not remain competitive as organizations or as a nation.

CAN THE DEMOGRAPHIC CHANGE HAPPENING BE STOPPED?

There are many people in our country who would like to stop the growth of our diverse population. That is not going to happen. With the reduction of America's white population, the growth of the Hispanic, Black, and Asian populations, as well as the migration of the world population, are all strong components to ensure that our diverse population will continue to grow. We have always taken in people from all over the world and this is not going to stop. As a matter of fact, with our declining white birth rate, it is an absolute necessity that we tap into the world's diverse population. We have gained the title of being "a nation of immigrants" honestly and this will continue. However, unlike in our past, the majority of our future immigrants will not be from Europe but from African, Asian, and Latino countries. These new entries will be essential to fulfill the needs of our future organizations.

For us to seriously think about sending five million young DACA workers and students back to countries with whom they have no connection is almost unthinkable. Here are five million potential future contributors to our society. They have been trained in our educational system and understand our norms and laws. Many have or are pursuing advanced degrees and we don't want to tap into that immense talent pool and future tax base. All I can say is, what are we thinking? I know it is an attempt by those who fear change or do not want the sharing of power to happen in our society but both of those things are inevitable. What we don't want to lose is the investment we have made in those five million DACA candidates and throw them out of our country just as they get to their productive years. The changing demographics of America are like a tsunami. It cannot be stopped. Our best strategy is to make this young population as strong and competitive as we can. Only then will our organizations and our nation as a whole, be able to maintain our competitive position in the future global economy. The current "replacement" theories of many Americans should not be a fear but a hope that it will happen, in order to fill the future void that will happen with the white male diminishing population.

THE WHITE MALE FUTURE PIPELINE

Many white Americans, in looking to the future, are making a stand to ensure that white males will still be the major source of our leadership pool that will continue allowing us to be a leader in the global economy. The thought is, if we as a nation can continue the development of our young white males that are in the pipeline, we as a nation will always have the white male leadership that has made our country the great one that it is today. However, there is a major factor that flies in the face of that thought process.

Let's take another look at that thought process and see how it holds up to the facts. We have stated before and is worth a reminder, that according to the U.S. Census Bureau that by 2060 white males will only represent twenty-nine percent of the American workforce. This indicates that clearly there will not be enough white males to fill the huge vacuum that will be created by the diminishing white male population. This, however, only tells half the story. A more revealing statistic states that in 1950, white males constituted thirty-seven percent of the entire population on the planet. It is now forecasted that by 2060, white males will only be nine percent of the planet's population. What this tells us is that there will be no large "white male pipeline" that can be tapped into and the option to pull from that pipeline for our future leaders will be very limited.

Of course, white males will always be a dominant factor in future leadership roles in our country but it tells us we can no longer turn our backs on developing leaders from our current and future population that will consist of women, people of color, gay and lesbian, transgender and disabled population. To do so, will put the future of our country in great peril.

MIXED-RACE CHILDREN

Another obvious change that we must accept is that with every future generation, there will be a growth of mixed-race children. With the end of segregation in our schools and social settings, it is natural that the mixing of races would occur. I mentioned before when growing up as the only "colored" child in my entire school class before I would go over to a new friend's house, I would be sure to ask if they had asked their parents if it was okay for me to come. Being blocked at the door several times by former white friends and I did not want to go through those uncomfortable moments of rejection again. To go from a time when a black child was unable to walk through a white family's front door to the number of mixed families today to me is astonishing. Commercials on television are now showing in great numbers, the reality of how many mixed marriages that exist today. No matter what your position is on the matter, the "browning of America" is a reality. There is no master plan to replace White males in our country but their sharing the future with people of different cultures is a reality.

Thirty or so years ago Time magazine had as a front foldout cover, a computer-generated picture of what the blending of all of our races would look like in five generations. In my opinion, I think the results were beautiful. The melting pot really produced some great-looking children. But in reality, it doesn't matter what I think or as a matter of fact, what you think as well. It is going to happen without our permission.

GETTING THE MOST FROM THE CHANGES THAT ARE OCCURRING

The more critical question is what should we be doing to maximize the benefits of these changes. It will take many generations, but if we start to work on equalizing the quality of education, we should be providing to all of our children; provide equal health care for all of them, provide them with the ability to seek higher levels of education without creating a lifetime of debt, give equal access to financing for people to secure homes and to create new businesses; we are on the path to a future strong America.

The remaining missing link is that we must not keep our future generations in the dark as to how our system works. We must teach them the rules of the system. Just think of what that could accomplish. If every American understood what they could do to reach their life's objectives and potential and did not look to the government to do it for them, think of the reduction that could be made to so many of our current government agencies. Instead of one central government trying to pull up three hundred and thirty million people (by 2080 that will be five hundred thirty-one million); but instead have those three hundred million and thirty million people growing and controlling their lives on their own, without the need for government help. With this change, crime will drop because more people will see a path to success without breaking the law. With this strategy, the middle class will again be able to flourish and grow. Socio-economic class differences will not be nullified but severely diminished and our population base will be able to spend more time being creative and productive instead of worrying about becoming homeless or, as we are seeing during the pandemic, able to feed themselves. We must remember that life is a game but in the case of our nation, it is a team game. We are all in this together. We must also remember that any team is only as strong as its weakest link. In the year 2020 and Covid has exposed some of the weak links that we have in our system and if ignored, will again be at our peril.

THE ADVANTAGE OF COMPETITION

Competition is healthy and it makes any individual and team stronger. I do believe in the quote that Ronald Reagan kept on his desk in the Oval Office. That was, "Without competition, you cannot have excellence." The fact is, if I do not have some force pushing me to become better, I will not become better. There are some who might suggest that the way to go is cooperation, not competition. They believe that creating a competitive environment causes friction, separation, backstabbing, and a drop in productivity. Of course, that is possible if there is no strong leadership to oversee that competitive environment. If greater co-operation is the goal of a team leader, then give rewards to the most co-operative people and watch co-operation among team members start to soar.

There are many examples that can be given to show that competition can be a good thing and can increase the level of excellence without major conflict. In our educational days, we were always competing for the highest grade in the class, and even those times that we didn't get it, there was no open animosity toward the student that beat us on that test. More than likely it just motivated you to try a little harder on the next one. We also see that the best students in the school, those who gain the honors of being summa or magna cum laude are usually praised and looked up to by the student body.

We see this also on a basketball team. If there are twelve players on the team, all will want to be one of the five who will start the game. If they are not one of the starters, watch the bench players in the last two minutes of an important and close game. The entire bench becomes the most enthusiastic cheerleaders in the arena. In the final huddle, those teammates who see something that a starter can do better will freely share that information, even though that advice may cement that starter's position even more. The reason that this dynamic is possible is simple; the players on the bench understand the rules of basketball and the skills they need to work on to gain a starting spot on the team. They know what they must work on to gain that starting role. They do not blame the person who is better than they are and every other player on the bench knows why they are not starting and what they need to do to improve their status. Again, a situation where the competition will produce better players and subsequently, a better team.

THE WHITE SUBURBAN MALE RESERVATION REVISITED

At this point, it might be important to point out again, one of the largest reservations that exist in our country is the white male reservation. Within that large reservation is a group of white, suburban, executives, managers, and professional employees. After their work day is over, just like people of all cultures, many elect to go directly to environments that contain only the people with whom they are comfortable. The only downside they might have in doing this their entire career is, they may quickly get out of touch with the people of our current and future work environments. With the rapidly changing demographics of our workforce and the increased momentum towards globalization, not getting more comfortable with their work team members, clients, and foreign contacts representing other cultures and races, they may soon become less effective in our rapidly changing world. Many white males are being jolted into reality by discovering that their new boss is a woman or a person of color. In the future, many white males might also find themselves managing departments where very few members of their team are people who look like them. Just like all "reservations," they can put you in a bubble and isolate you from the realities of the world.

It is becoming more difficult in today's world to only operate in your limited comfortable environments and still be successful in an increasingly diverse world. The future requirement will be that the mainstream American rules will fall on every individual's shoulders and will require everyone to make some adaptations. There will be no exceptions, not even for that white male who wishes and chooses to remain comfortably on his reservation.

THE IMPACT OF THE WHITE SUBURBAN MALE RESERVATION ON OUR FUTURE

It is important to once more reiterate that, if you are a white male living in suburbia, it does not necessarily mean that you are operating in mainstream America. Having white skin and living in a suburban community does not mean you have melted. It could simply mean that you live and socialize with other white males (and your white significant other) and in many cases, only white males, on your reservation. If you are a white male, your former ethnic forefathers might have made the journey from your ethnic community to a point where you are no longer seen as Irish, Polish, Greek, Russian, or Italian. You are now simply seen as white or as, just an American. But the reality is, many may have stopped their journey short of the mainstream. If you are still mentally on the white male reservation, it may keep you from seeing the reality of what America is becoming. If you are not becoming comfortable with all elements of our changing population, you may have just shut yourself down to the multi-cultural world as it is and will continue to be. No matter what race, religion, ethnic background, or sexual orientation with which you identify as an individual, we all have a choice with regard to the level of commitment we want to give to playing by the rules of the various cultural environments in which we live. However, for a person to make that choice wisely, the mainstream business rules must be shared with them so that they can make an informed personal choice. I have found that when you tell anyone who wants to succeed in business, that they must eventually embrace the mainstream rules of business no matter who they are, it makes the choice to play by mainstream rules less emotional for them. It becomes easier when they know that they are not alone in having to make this effort.

When you play effectively by mainstream rules, you can be successful in a mainstream organization and, as a result, will be able to share mainstream rewards. This realization becomes a powerful motivating factor to get people to leave their mental reservations and eventually become contributors to the organization's mission at a higher level. Understanding the rules will also make a person a better candidate for future upper executive positions. We have stated before that you can't play any game effectively if you don't know the rules of that game, but even more fundamentally, without knowledge of the game's rules, you are unable to make the decision whether you want to play by them or not. Let's teach the rules to everyone and level the playing field for all.

The more our diverse workforce decides to join the mainstream game in greater numbers, the more the white male will be forced to live in a diverse world. Looking at scientific studies and numerical facts, we have already made the case that this advancement of demographic change cannot be stopped. It is inevitable.

Of course, we are currently going through a time when many White Americans are trying their best to slow down if not stop the future distribution of power. Tactics like establishing voting restrictions, keeping substandard schools in emerging cultural communities, not having an equal and fair distribution of money for advance education costs, not having available funds for starting new businesses, and the gerrymandering of voting districts are all meant to maintain the white male power structure.

When will we start to comprehend that the development of our entire population will reflect how competitive we can make our future workforce? My hope is that it does not take too long for us to figure this out, our future generations deserve more from all of us.

CHAPTER EIGHTEEN

CHARTING OUR PROGRESS

THE PROGRESS AFRICAN-AMERICANS HAVE MADE

Although I am talking about the future and the challenges that lie ahead for us as a nation, I am not suggesting that progress has not been made. The advantage of being able to hang around as long as I have has allowed me to chart firsthand some of this progress. Let's take a quick look at just a few areas where progress in societal acceptance can be seen.

SPORTS

Growing up in the forties and fifties as an African-American, I have personally been a witness to how far our country has changed in just my lifetime. I do remember gathering around the radio with my brothers listening to the play of Jackie Robinson, the first Negro to play professional baseball on a white team. It was hard for us to believe that he would be allowed to do so and that he was so good. It not only gave us a vast sense of pride but also gave us the go signal to try to compete in the white world.

In football, the "firsts" include the first players in the "white" league, the first black players to play on a southern team, the first black quarterback, and the first black coach to manage a professional team. In looking at these sports today, it is hard to imagine that we as a nation had to struggle with those issues for so long.

POLITICS

Not counting Reconstruction, major advancements of African-Americans in politics would include: Thurgood Marshall, the first Black Supreme Court Justice; Douglas Wilder, the first Black Governor of a state; Shirley Chisholm, the first Black woman elected to Congress and to run for President; Robert Weaver, the first Black Cabinet Member; General Colin Powell, the first Black Chairman of the Joint Chief of Staff; Andrew Young, the first Black Ambassador to the U.N.; Kamala Harris, the first Black and Indian women Vice President; and of course, our first Black President, Barack Obama.

It is important to note that I am only tracking the progress of African-Americans. Progress reports can and should be noted for women, Hispanic, Asian, Native Americans, and people of different sexual orientations. All have made progress at different rates of speed but progress is being made by all groups.

ENTERTAINMENT

Like all areas of American life, I have been able to personally live through the progress we have made racially in the entertainment arena. I can remember the Nat King Cole television show, the first hosted by a black man on a major network in 1956. His show was not broadcasted to all southern states. Or the 1957 movie "Island in the Sun" starring Harry Belafonte and Dorothy Dandridge, both black actors, who were not allowed to touch other white stars in their intimate love scenes. The movie created a national uproar. We can clearly see the societal change of attitudes in this area with today's t.v. shows and movies.

HATE GROUP ACTIVITY

Although we are currently seeing the rise of hate groups in our country, it was a lot worse eighty years ago. I mentioned the crosses burned on the lawns of three houses for being the first black to move into a white neighborhood. Although it happened a little ahead of my time, we all have seen pictures of the 1925 White supremacist rally in Washington D.C. when 30,000 clan members, all with KKK white sheets, marched in a parade. Although white supremacist rallies still occur like the 2017, one held in Charlottesville Va., the numbers were smaller and the white robes had disappeared. They were replaced with blazing tike torches. I'm sure they were sensitive to what the public reaction would be too wearing white robes. Can we list that as progress? We could until January 6th, 2021. With the raid on the U.S. Capitol building, we were reminded that White Supremacy is alive and well in our country. Many have said that white hatred had never gone away, it had just gone underground. Well, we no longer have to debate this issue any longer, as of January 6th white hate groups are no longer underground. They are now in full view.

Unfortunately, we cannot say that incidents of police brutality have declined in any significant way as well. With today's cell phone video capabilities and police auto cams, we have far too many documented events where police brutality is still taking place. Hopefully, greater progress can be made in this area in the future.

To reach the state of utopia, where we just see people as people, and when our evaluation of them goes much deeper than race, gender, and sexual orientation, is generations away. But if we continue to make progress in helping more people to get to the mainstream and if more people decide that they want to play in the mainstream game, the faster that state of utopia will happen. Getting to that objective faster and with less difficulty will depend on future laws, political attitudes, social interactions and peer attitudes toward respecting and accepting each other.

THE CASE FOR LEAVING RESERVATIONS AND JOINING THE MAINSTREAM CHOICES FOR INDIVIDUALS

Being accepted into mainstream America by mainstream Americans is only half the battle for our nation's efforts to increase our mainstream population. The other major challenge is to get enough Americans to mentally leave their cultural reservations and even attempt to play in our country's mainstream. Let's take a look at some of the pros and cons that should be reviewed if you are considering jumping into the mainstream competition.

On the down or challenging side, first and foremost, when you leave your community to go to mainstream America, you are leaving a world that you know and love. You are leaving your comfortable environments, your security, your roots, and many of the activities and people to which you want to stay close. Add to that, in entering the mainstream, you will often be going into worlds and environments that might make you feel inadequate because many of the environments and activities will be new to you.

Also, if you find yourself in an activity that is being conducted within the white male reservation, you will more than likely be in a small minority if you are a person of color. You might also feel spotlighted and the center of everyone's attention. This would also apply to a woman that has wondered into a white male reservation environment or event. This might occur on the golf course or at any after-work bar gathering. In these situations, it might cause you to be very reserved and cautious to ensure that you do not say or do the wrong thing. This feeling of inadequacy is of course short-lived because learning and executing "white male reservation's rules" is not a difficult thing to learn and put into practice. We're not talking about things that are very complicated. Adapting to the white male reservation's way of life is not a big deal as it will not take you long to become comfortable with their environmental requirements.

As for the new people you will meet, I have found that they will soon become comfortable with you when you become comfortable with them and their surroundings. The moment you become "fluent" in any given environment, the spotlight goes away and you can then enjoy the people and the event in which you find yourself. This all comes about naturally in time. Much more important, they will get to know "the real" you when you are no longer concerned about not fitting in. This is the time when you can become your "Authentic" self, you can then relax and have some fun.

Remember, getting comfortable on the white male reservation is only a temporary step on your journey to mainstream America. White males who have made the transition from the white male reservation to the mainstream will not see you as a culturally different person because these will be people who have not barricaded themselves from the changing world. Because they have chosen to live their life in the American mainstream, they will have grown use to and comfortable with diversity. They are the white males who have the ability to see beyond skin color and gender.

You will notice the difference between a white male reservation event and a mainstream American event as soon as you walk into a room. Only events that are held with people who have not mainstreamed, will that feeling of being an intruder occur. However, if you attend "white only" environments often enough, eventually, they will become second nature to you. You will soon be able to not give those occasions a second thought. It's just like learning a new language.

The more often you use a language, the better you will be able to speak it. This is true with penetrating the White male reservation as well. The more activities that you attend in the white reservation, the more comfortable you will become. This will lead to you being more accepting of those people with whom you are communicating and finally lead to you becoming more comfortable with that group. In reality, you are actually contributing to helping that group move a little further toward the mainstream. It will be the first step for some in that room to have social interaction with someone outside of their reservation.

A LOOK AT THE POSITIVE SIDE OF JOINING THE MAINSTREAM

Jumping into the mainstream is not for the weak at heart. For in doing so, it will take you on new and strange adventures. It will force you into learning new activities, meet new people and force you to take on new challenges. It cannot be said often enough, just because you work in a major corporation or large government agency does not qualify you as a mainstream player. You merely have a job in a mainstream organization.

The mainstream activities that we are referring to are those actions and activities that occur outside of the normal 9 to 5 working hours and usually not at the office building. If you have upper management or executive ambitions, they may require you to learn new activities such as bridge, chess, golf, tennis, skiing, sailing, or attending artistic events such as ballets, symphonies, operas, Broadway musicals, and cocktail parties. This would include attending all organizational functions such as retirement and promotion parties and annual office parties.

The game may also ask you to do community work such as volunteering for committee and board work with organizations like the Jr. Chamber of Commerce, the Chamber of Commerce, and/or the United Way. The specific activity is not as important as the people with whom you will interact when you participate in that activity. In deciding what new activities to take up, it should be based on what you think would be fun and what might be in the interest of the upper management team in your organization. If they are a bunch of golfers, that might be a good choice. If everyone attends the local symphony performances, you might consider doing that as well. You have choices, so you might as well start something that you will like doing. I have found that whatever you choose, your interest will move from frustration to mild interest to, in many cases, pushing you to become a fanatic. That has happened many times to me.

The fun you will have learning the new activity however is just a plus. The major purpose for your participation in those activities will be the new people you will meet. When people meet you in a relaxed social setting and do what they like to do with you, your relationship with that person may take on a deeper bond and a stronger connection. And so, the obvious advantage of learning mainstream activities is that it connects you with mainstream people who may be in a position to sponsor your career or at a minimum, give you helpful advice. That has happened to me via the activities of golf, tennis, skiing, bridge, ballet, and volunteer work. All have allowed me to meet people who have in turn helped me with my business growth.

BY MAINSTREAMING, ARE WE TURNING OUR BACK ON OUR CULTURE?

We all have heard the statement "You should never forget where you came from." From my youth, I have always heard the adults around me judging all successful "colored people" on whether that successful person gave something back to the community. The more that person contributed to the Black struggled, the more that person was respected.

We all give back. It may be in the form of $1.00 in church, being a member of the PTA, a scout leader, or making a $100,000 donation to your local ballet company. We give back because it is built into the rules of the game. From the days three hundred years ago when the Royal families of Europe sponsored the great composers of that time, to the contributions of the first U.S. tycoons that gave us the Mellon Museums and Carnegie Libraries, to today's wealthy class like Bill and Malinda Gates that give billions to charities. We can see that giving back is a baked in rule.

The key to giving back is deciding what can be given in time and money at any given period in your life. The hope is that if you play the game effectively, you may be able to give back much more than if you did not play the mainstream game. This was the case with Charles Curtis, a Native American and member of the Kaw Nation. When he was young, he chose to live with his white grandparents instead of staying on his reservation. As a result of his decision to join the mainstream, he eventually became our nation's first Native American U.S. congressman, senator, and Vice President under Herbert Hoover.

A great recent example is Deb Haaland, a Native American who was recently appointed to President Biden's cabinet as Secretary of the Interior. She has always been a community activist and a supporter of climate control, environmental issues, and protector of Indigenous land. I would imagine that by playing the game and Becoming a cabinet member, she can now make a much greater impact in her areas of interest than she would as a tribal activist. The same can be said of former President Obama and his beginning role as a community activist. I am confident in saying that his contribution to our nation, even if he would have made an impact as a community developer, was far more valuable as President than it would have been if he had stayed in his neighborhood.

Another benefit of joining the mainstream game is that you become more aware of the dynamics that are going on in your organization. Even if you do not want an upward-oriented career, knowledge of how the system works makes you much more effective as you compete for resources, job assignments, raises, and bonuses. The six o'clock news will even take on a new perspective because of your knowledge of the rules. With knowledge of the system you can better direct your career but equally important, can help the people around you including members of your family. The best coaches are those who thoroughly know the rules of the game they are coaching.

A final benefit that must be mentioned is the rewards that are given to mainstream players. It is natural if the people at the top of any pyramid have the right to make the rules, that those people would pass out the rewards of money and position to individuals who play by their rules. I know I do in my company and will strongly suggest that you might do so as well. It then stands to reason if a person wants to be rewarded with mainstream positions and wealth that they must make the choice to play by mainstream rules. Not only that, it must be remembered that there is competition out there. Others will be seeking the same positions and wealth you desire. This will require your best effort if you expect to win. After all, it is a game.

The key to all of these benefits happening is you must play by the "unwritten rules" of our mainstream system. The system will give you enough space to define your uniqueness, and your special talents and give you an opportunity to live out your choices in life. It is incumbent on each one of us to learn the "unwritten rules" and then execute our lives by those rules to the best of our ability if we are to reach the goals we have set for ourselves.

STAYING ON YOUR CULTURAL RESERVATION

As we have stated before, the game is defined by individual choices. In a free society such as ours, that freedom of choice must be extended to everyone. That means that if someone in your community is playing by mainstream rules and not the rules of your cultural group, don't label them as a "sell-out." They have made a choice as to which of the environments they would like to compete in and are doing what they need to do to succeed in that environment. If you want to be successful in France, you don't speak German. "When in the mainstream, you do what mainstream people do."

If your resentment is based on envy, just try to remember that you have that same choice. I personally feel that my life is more than I can handle on any given day. I just don't have the time nor interest to live other people's lives as well. Again, that individual is merely practicing the freedom for which generations of his ancestors have fought and many have died, for him to do. I have often wondered what Dr. King, who died for our right to compete in mainstream America, would think if he returned and saw the reluctance of so many African-Americans that are using their freedom of choose to remain on the Black reservation. I would have to imagine that he might question if his death was worth the small numbers of us who have chosen to play in the mainstream game.

A better strategy in addressing a person who has made the decision to play the mainstream game is to give encouragement to that individual and wish him or her well. Who knows, you may need a mainstream friend later on in your career.

CHAPTER NINETEEN

FINAL THOUGHTS ON WHAT LIES AHEAD

A REVIEW OF SOME OF OUR MAJOR DISCUSSIONS

We are at a crossroads as a nation, as organizations, and as individuals. Since our future will heavily be based on the choices we are currently making today, here are some final thoughts about the things that we should consider in making those choices.

CHOICES THAT ORGANIZATIONS NEED TO CONSIDER

The major choice with which we are confronted as a nation is to believe or not believe that the world is changing in the areas of globalization and our internal changing demographics. It is incumbent upon us to accurately predict the impact that either or both will have on our future. If we believe that dramatic change is upon us, then we must prepare our organizations for the realities of competing in a much more competitive world. Within this competitive environment, we will have a much more diverse workforce which may be totally polarized politically and culturally. If so, then our course of action and action steps are clear.

We must develop our high potential diverse and women leaders to equip them with the knowledge and skills needed to lead at higher levels. This must include openly and honestly sharing the requirements of executive leadership. We must then help them through the personal changes that will be required of them to be effective in higher leadership positions.

A second major challenge is to create a work environment that will defuse the divisions that currently exist and will continually grow if not addressed. This will require awareness and sensitivity training to the degree it was implemented shortly after the passage of the Civil Rights Act and the early diversification of our workforce. At that time, this training went a long way to build bridges of understanding between individuals and groups that had never before worked together. We stopped that training for the most part two generations ago simply because we felt it was no longer needed. We honestly thought that race relations in our country had improved to the point that racial bigotry and deep political divisions were no longer an organizational problem. With current events, we now can see that we have made a great miscalculation. Not only must this training be reconstructed but we must also provide other communication forums to allow associates to discuss their feelings and concerns.

DOES AWARENESS TRAINING WORK?

I helped to write IBM's first "Black Awareness" training session, the first in the country, in 1967. It was shortly after the Civil Rights Act of 1964 was past and companies were beginning to implement their first Affirmative Action programs. IBM's strategy was to hold town meetings around the country to announce the new policies. The ground rules at the town meetings were to have no restrictions on anyone's comments or questions. Everything said at that meeting was not to be recorded or held against any employee. It was also stated that the moment the meeting was over; any violations of the new policy would result in immediate dismissal. This was the session where everyone could get everything out of their system. My section of the country was south of the Mason-Dixon Line and east of the Mississippi River. This of course included all of the great states of the former confederacy.

The "N" word was used so often that by the end of my sessions it was something I didn't hear or to which I even reacted. I called myself a spear catcher because of the types of questions I was asked. Some of the extreme ones included, "Does your skin color rub off on your sheets when you sleep at night?" Why do you live with rats and roaches?" "Do Black men really have tails?" That is the level of ignorance as it related to race knowledge and sensitivity that prevailed in 1967.

Of course, with sixty years of contact via school integration and equal opportunity work laws, we have come a long way in dispelling much of that ignorance. There is no doubt in my mind that awareness and sensitivity training played a major role in advancing the mindset of all American workers. To think about where we were then with race and gender attitudes is almost laughable. That training has taken us a long way from where we started, however, I would still venture a guess that we currently need many more forums for discussion to allow people to be able to discuss current race, gender, religious, and sexual orientation issues to move us forward from where we are today. And if anyone is wondering about the answers to the questions above, it is "NO" about the sheets and tails.

KEEPING POLITICAL OPINIONS TO YOURSELF

Freedom of speech is one of the basic freedoms that we cherish in our country. Political freedom is also one of the basic freedoms that we also enjoy and have fought to ensure that it is not infringed upon. However, in the workplace the two when put together might not be a wise thing to do. With today's extreme left and extreme right political points of view, emotions can run so high; it is almost impossible for some individuals to let it not affect their opinions of people with opposite political views. Even mentioning support for a political movement or the name of a political figure, as we are seeing, can drive a wedge between two people.

How then can we prevent the deep feelings about political views from effecting relationships at work and even more importantly team effectiveness? For one, just don't talk politics at work. If someone brings up a political topic that isn't connected to the work mission, tell them that work is not the place to talk about that subject. The deeper someone goes into a political topic that others disagree with, the greater the chance it will have a negative impact on a work environment. While we're at it, discussions about religion should also be added to that list of don't do.

Another thing that might be considered to lessen friction among peers is a moderated discussion among employees if those divisions have surfaced and some resolution of the tension must be reached. In these discussions, the moderator must remain neutral and not allow personal attacks to take place. The purpose is to get both sides to understand the thinking of the opposite point of view and to reestablish a human connection away from political views. The best way to start those discussions is to talk about the things that the two individuals or groups have in common. Once that foundation has been laid, addressing the issues of difference will not be as severe.

BEING A MENTOR IN A DIVERSE WORLD

We must also be more aggressive in our mentoring efforts. Realized that many organizations have in place formal mentoring programs but they are truly formal. When I say move forward in an aggressive manner is to have mentors be more personal in informing mentees about the realities of moving up in our system. It would also include helping those mentees come to grips with some of the negative emotions with which they must deal if their choice is to move their career to a higher level. I guess I'm saying that mentors must just "tell it like it is." I think the current political term is "full disclosure." We can no longer afford to soft-peddle the truth about what it takes to prepare oneself for executive leadership positions. Mentoring messages must be honest and straight forward even at the risk of sharing information that might be uncomfortable and unpopular with their protégé. Being afraid to tell a high potential Black mentee a requirement that you think will conflict with their Black culture is sending that person to their career advancement doom.

Even when leveling with that candidate, that mentor must also "walk a mile" in that protégé's shoes and suggest helpful solutions to aid in the struggles that they might have with their conflicts. This may require interactions that go beyond the four walls of their office in a one-hour talk on Friday afternoon. It may require social interactions like inviting them to go to the ballet, play golf or invite them to your Saturday night cocktail party. Just throwing out the advice of "work hard and you'll get ahead" is no longer an acceptable standard for mentoring in a diverse world.

WHO IS RESPONSIBLE FOR CHANGE: THE ORGANIZATION OR THE INDIVIDUAL?

Of course, both are responsible to change especially in changing times. Remember, "when you're through changing, you are through." This applies to both the organization as well as to any individual. If you want immediate results, however, we must be practical. Value experts have claimed that it takes an individual two to three years to change a value system within themselves. With repetition and dedication to the effort, a person can learn new values very much like learning a new language. After a period of consistently using that language, they no longer have to think about it. It becomes a part of their DNA and will operate in their subconscious thought processes.

The change of a value system in an organization will take a lot longer. Fluency of a value in organizations can be measured when people enter an office building and without consciously thinking about it, conduct themselves in an acceptable manner that the organization demands of them. A good example of how long it takes to change an organizational value can be seen in the area of safety on the job. A factory does not become safer simply because the executive team announces a new safety policy. It takes years of talking about it in a staff meeting, safety films being shown, posters, pamphlets, and repeating the policy until "blue in the face." Maybe after years of making these measures, the message sinks in and the accidents start to lessen. The organization must become fluent and depending on the size of the organization it could take years. In an organization of fifty thousand people with constant turnover, it could take as long as ten to twenty years to have those safety procedures become "that's just how we do it around here." The intensity of effort that the leadership team brings to the issue will also dictate the length of time of that new value system's implementation.

Implementing values such as Diversity and Inclusion principles, developing mutual respect among peers and teamwork are examples of values that cannot be changed by memos and a two-hour training class. True cultural value change in an organization takes a lot of effort from the executive and management team constantly speaking to the new values but more importantly openly showing those new values in their daily actions. Leadership by example really works. We should never forget the rule that a picture is always worth a thousand words.

For a nation of over three hundred million people, getting our country to change its values will take many, many generations. Issues such as women's rights, equal justice, and racial equality will not be resolved in one's lifetime. If you expect the system to change in your life time to one that will except you just as you are, forget it. The only way you can reap the benefits of our system in your life is to change yourself. If you compare your ability to adapt in two to three years and your organization's ability to change a little in fifteen to thirty years, it is clear who has to shoulder most of the work in changing for your good. It is you!

Want some more depressing news? If you're thinking about the rules of the entire system changing just for you, remember the system has been around for over eight hundred years and the world has pretty much bought into them. Maybe there could be significant changes in the global system (i.e. we lose the battle for democracy and free enterprise to Fascist dictators) in the next five hundred years, but we won't be around to voice our disapproval. The bottom line is, it all boils down to; if you want to enjoy the fruits of success in your lifetime and there are changes that have to be made, you will be the entity that will have to make them.

Of course, the system is always looking for individuals who are trying to improve the system, but this is expected to be done within the rules of the current system. History has shown that those who try to make a radical change to the system by completely overhauling it have usually paid a tremendous price for doing so. Some would include Jesus, Spartacus, Mahatma Gandhi, John Brown, Abraham Lincoln, Martin Luther King, and a long list of others. Thank heavens for all of them because they all made our system a better one but they all paid the ultimate price for doing so. And so if we don't personally want to go to those extremes, we can still make a difference by working to improve things by working within the system's rules. Of course, to do this will require understanding what those rules are.

From an organizational perspective, it means that the more people who are helped in accepting and then begin playing by the organization's rules, the faster all of the future challenges that the organization must face, can be addressed with an effective team. Critical future issues must be attacked by a larger pool of people who all have a common understanding of the mission and a common language that they can use to address any and all issues with their diverse teammates.

If on the other hand, an organization chooses to not think strategically and does nothing about adapting to the current changes in the country's demographics or their work population, they must be prepared to take on increased employee turnover due to career frustrations, an increase in the number of employee HR disputes that will likely occur and in today's climate of division, even possible employee violence. At a minimum, there will be less effective team co-operation. All of this will, of course, lead to having a major impact on accomplishing the organization's mission and/or bottom-line targets. We must face the reality that we have an emotionally divided nation that for many will not be turned off when they get to their place of work. This is something that must be resolved. Ignoring it could be very costly for any organization.

CHOICES THAT INDIVIDUALS NEED TO CONSIDER

As individuals, we have the ability to take control of our destiny through the choices that we make. The major obstacles to gaining this control are two-fold. The first is to figure out what we want to do. This includes such issues as, how high do we want to rise in our organization and deciding what will make us happy. This is so difficult that many people do not figure it out their entire careers. Of course, if you don't know what you want out of a career, all the choices that you are making become meaningless as they will not direct you to any set or known objective. To quote the wise hare in Alice in wonderland when asked, "How do I get out of here?" His reply was, "It all depends on where you want to go." There is also an old adage that tells us, "If you don't know where you are going, you might end up someplace else." It still applies to all of us as we think about our careers. Setting a career objective is a difficult decision to make but the sooner it is made, the faster you will get there. By the way, if you get it wrong the first time, you can always change it. The faster you set even that wrong career objective, the faster you will learn that it is wrong, get out of it and move on to better things.

Once you have set a career or life objective and decide to enter "the game," the choices you make will allow you to reach them. We have already made the case that all of us have 100% control of all of our decisions. But there is another barrier. That barrier is, in order to make the correct choice, one must understand how the system works. You really do have to play the game by the game's rules to reach your objectives. You must learn the "unwritten rule" of our system and your organization as well, by understanding the dues that must be paid in order to make the correct choices for your individual goals. This is the only way you can determine what the right moves are for you. This is how we can maximize that hundred percent control that we all have. To have that control but make the wrong choices simply because you didn't know all of your options and their consequences, is not a good thing.

Once you have determined your personal life objectives, you are then in the position of determining what game board will allow you to reach those goals. The options are whether you want and need to be a player on your racial, ethnic, religious, or sexual orientation "reservation" or do your objectives require that you become a player in the American mainstream. Remember, there is no good or bad, right or wrong choice in this regard. The good and right choice is the one that makes you, as an individual, happy.

It is important to remember that the mere fact that you go to a mainstream job in a mainstream organization does not mean that you are a mainstream player. In that situation, you have the opportunity to be one but if you do not play by the rules of your organization or in essence what I am calling the organizational game, while in that job, you then merely have a job, not a career.

If you want to compete for and achieve higher-level positions, you must play effectively by American mainstream organizational rules.

IF I'M A GAME PLAYER, WHEN DO I BECOME AN AMERICAN?

To be recognized as an American can be done by simply defining it as a place where someone lives. If you live in the geographical area that is defined as America and you take the necessary steps to become a citizen, then you are an American. But we are a tribal-oriented nation and many of our citizens live on their respective reservations. As mentioned before, these reservations are numerous. They are usually formed when people of like cultures and interests come together as a community. This may have been forced upon them by our society via laws that were passed when we formed Native American and African-American reservations; or by choice, as was done by the Irish, Jewish and Italian communities. No matter how they came to be, after generations, most people that live on their reservations are comfortable in doing so. Even if it might not be the best of worlds for them, it is none the less, their world and until they can figure out a way to leave it, it is the only world they know. For many it is home and they have no desire or intentions of leaving.

This is the reason we break Americans into sub-categories. Those sub-categories are for those people who have their own geographical borders within America's boundaries. This would include such geographically enclosed communities as Native Americans, Black Americans, Hispanic Americans (divided into many sub-cultures such as the Cuban, Mexican, and Puerto Rican communities), Asian Americans (some of their sub-cultures being Japanese, Chinese, Korean Vietnamese and others), White Americans (Irish, German, English, etc.), Gay and Lesbian Americans (and the list goes on).

It is important to repeat, however, that those physical boundaries are not the most restrictive reservations on which we can be contained. The most difficult boundaries that must be penetrated for an individual to reach mainstream America are those that are mental. These are difficult because it forces a person to confront change. Thoughts that begin with, "But I don't like to ....," "But I don't want to....," "But I shouldn't have to...," "It isn't right to have to...," "It's not fair that I should have to...." (and this list goes on as well). They all define the mental restrictions we erect in trying to convince ourselves that we have the right not to change.

If we do decide to change, this change cannot just be at the surface level. We can easily move our furniture to a house that is located in suburbia but it is much more difficult to release our minds to be open to new and challenging environments and activities. If you choose hanging out with your cultural friends rather than going to your boss's cocktail party simply because you might be uncomfortable, it makes those choices important career decisions. If you don't go to that cocktail party, even when you know that it will help you reach your life objectives, then it is fair to say that you are mentally stuck on your reservation. Again, this is ok if you can accept the results that go with that choice.

To answer the question as to when do we become an American. That is an easy one. You are an American if you are an American citizen. A more pointed question might be, "When do I think of myself as an American, who happens to be Black rather than "I'm a Black American?" That goes a long way to let you evaluate for yourself, where you might be on your journey to Mainstream America. It's a question that only you can answer for yourself. Of course, that test applies to every group which would include all races, religions, ethnic and sexual orientation groups.

CHAPTER TWENTY

IMPORTANT SKILLS TO CONSIDER ON YOUR JOURNEY

Before leaving you, I have always been told never to bring up a problem or a challenge without also suggesting a solution. In honoring that "unwritten" rule, may I offer some of the skills and strategies, along with some recommendations you might want to consider. I have tried to separate our challenges into three groupings, Our Nation, Our Organizations, and as Individuals.

In my first book, **Empowering Yourself: The Organizational Game Revealed, The Best Kept Secret in Organizational America,** I not only described how our system works, but I also defined three of the most important skills that are required to be effective within our system. These skills are **Emotional Control, Delegation, and Strategic Thinking.** Let's examine how each of those skills will impact our future.

EMOTIONAL CONTROL: *OUR NATION*

There is no doubt that we are going through some very emotional times as a nation today. Issues such as abortion, police violence, voting rights, educational strategies, book banning, inflation, health care, sexual orientation, transgender discussions, school curriculum, child care, equal justice, gun control, election denying, tuition paybacks, environment and climate control (you can stop me at any time) and so many other issues that I'm sure you could add significantly to the list. Many of these issues have gone from not just being protested, but many have the potential of exploding into violence, some having already done so.

As a nation, we must find ways to step back to get our emotions under control. The "unwritten rule" of counting to ten before you act or speak clearly applies to us, we the people, in today's national climate.

RECOMMENDATIONS

The best way to accomplish this is to begin to dialogue these issues in more open forums. Talking openly about any subject is like stem escaping from a tea kettle. The water is still hot but the kettle won't explode because of the release of pressure. Discussion requires an exchange of information and facts that, if emotions can be controlled, could change minds or at a minimum lead to compromise. These discussions can occur in neighborhood groups, PTA organizations, Home Associations as well as our classrooms. Of course, any session should have specific guidelines, codes of conduct, and skilled moderators to conduct the sessions. This is a skill that all of us hope that our representatives in Congress will discover soon because to continue on their emotional tribal paths, means that we will continually stay an extremely divided nation with very few of our important issues being resolved.

EMOTIONAL CONTROL: *OUR ORGANIZATIONS*

As with our nation, our organizations must deal with all the above issues that their employees bring emotionally into the workplace. However, the issue for organizations becomes less philosophical and more real-time for they must deal with workplace issues on a daily basis. These issues must be detected and resolved before they escalate into emotional confrontations.

Of course, with the availability and open carry laws, guns and workplace violence prevention will be on full alert. Having more avenues available for employees to report, discuss, and defuse emotional situations will be paramount to the reduction and prevention of these situations.

RECOMMENDATIONS

Suggestion boxes, open door policies, poster campaigns, agenda items in management and employee training sessions, box lunch discussions on the various topics, specific policy and practice statements entered into organizational literature, executive messaging, finding best practices of other organizations and other measures must now be considered a greater priority by the executive team.

With the added environmental changes that are affecting most organizations today such as Covid recovery, work-at-home issues, the organization stands on political issues, the fluctuation of the job market, demands of boards and stockholders, and issues of developing a diverse workforce, all leads to added pressure on today's the executive teams. Addressing these pressure situations will require today's executives to stay calm, collect factual data on every situation, collaborate with diverse people and diverse opinions, and make decisions that are as emotionally free as possible.

It is also important that C-suite members and the executive team start to put these issues on their agencies to ensure that the messaging that comes from that group has a common tone and an understanding of conduct guidelines. Of course, all individuals of the executive team will not be in agreement on many of the issues listed above but everyone should show that the organization has a united message that sets the environmental cultural of the organization. This might take a weekend retreat to accomplish this, but could be time well spent. It might also help resolve some of the differences that might exist between members of the executive team. Even if that message is merely that we don't discuss political issues at work outside of those that have been included in our policy statements. It is something that is best to spelled out clearly for all to understand and with which they can become comfortable.

EMOTIONAL CONTROL: *THE INDIVIDUAL*

This, as I state in my **Empowering Yourself** book, is by far the most difficult skill to master. Why? Simply because we are human. As we can get very emotional with an issue that is close to home and affect us personally.

We can recite many of the unwritten rules that cover this issue without a second thought. "Count to ten," "Turn the other check," "Get control of your hot buttons," and "Do unto others as you would have them do to you" (Golden advice by the way). But we also know all of those are easier said than done.

RECOMMENDATIONS

The best advice that I can give on this issue (for this is a personal struggle that is different for each of us) is to get to know your own personal "hot buttons" and prevent not having them triggered when someone pushes one of them. This, of course, takes time, a lot of practice, and feedback from family and friends to accomplish, but it is truly worth the effort. It is fairly well known that many decisions that are made under stress and emotion are ones that you might later regret. My mantra in this area is to utter to myself two statements. "Never be rude" and "Fly like an Eagle."

They are effective for me because if I want to lash out at someone to draw blood and hope that it will hurt them, I have concluded that it would be rude to do so. A reminder to myself that I shouldn't be rude helps me in those situations to get control of my responses. It's my "count to ten before you speak" control.

"Fly like and Eagle" is a reminder when I get emotional, I should simply rise above the situation with which I'm confronted and try to take a wider and broader view of that situation. At a higher elevation, you might even be able to walk that mile from the other person's viewpoint and start a non-emotional, constructive conversation with that individual or even a group.

Have I mastered this skill? Of course not. But over the years, it has allowed me to get better at this most difficult skill. Once you do rise above the emotional fray, remember people will try to hit your hot buttons, but don't allow them to bring you back to their level of emotion. That does no-one any good, especially you. By not striking verbally back is in essence, turning an emotional cheek. Even if no other party is involved and you are just making decisions about your family, your job, your future, and any other decision that only you are required to make: don't do it in an emotional state. Those are the decisions that we will often regret.

DELEGATION: *THE NATION*

Delegation is a skill that can have two important benefits. One, it can free you up to do multiple things and often allow you to concentrate on more important items that you need to accomplish; and two, it can be an excellent tool to pass on information and to grow and motivate people.

For this to be utilized as a nation is the core of our democratic process. It is impossible for us as individuals to address massive problems such as climate control, gun safety, and public health issues but we can and expect our legislative representatives to do it for us. We, in essence, delegate our elected officials to do the will of the people of which we are one. Sometimes this works and sometimes it does not, but it is still available to us. If we do not exercise this skill, or in this case, this right, we put ourselves in a situation where we must live with what we get without having input. Bottom-line is we must make our positions and voices known to our government through messaging and voting or, just live with the consequences.

DELEGATION: *THE ORGANIZATION*

Executives are very familiar with the skill and/or art of delegation. It is a key skill that had to be learned for them to even get to a high leadership position. The saying that "stuff" always flow downhill is merely telling us that whoever is at the top of a pyramid has the right to make the rules and expect that their rules will be shared and enforced by people lower in the organization. These rules might include policy decisions, product and marketing decisions, organizational value policies and all decisions that will affect the mission and/or bottom-line of their organization. Usually, these decisions are made by a group of an inner circle (i.e., the C-suite in business) but they must be implemented by delegating them down through the organization. How effectively they will be implemented will depend on such things as motivation levels, management skills, communication channels in place, clarity of the policy, and how effective follow-up procedures are implemented.

DELEGATION: *THE INDIVIDUAL*

All of the benefits that are gained by executives when they delegate can apply to us as individuals if we can master this skill. I'm sure one can quickly conclude that yes if I had a staff of people I would be a great delegator. Of course, this is a true statement but don't let that stop you. I make the claim that we all are CEO's of our own lives and it is important to take this seriously. Freeing ourselves up to do the important things in our lives and careers can be done without an extensive staff and overhead.

Sometimes we are delegating and not labeling it as such. For example, if you have a tax firm fill out your taxes, you have just delegated. Having one of your parents watch your children when you have other things to do is an act of delegation. How about when one of your children or a neighbor's child cuts your lawn, if so you have just delegated. Even when you pick up the family meal at the local supermarket instead of cooking it yourself on any given night is an act of delegation. How effective you can be on the job or at home in implementing this skill will not only have an effect on your ability to focus on the more important projects in your life but can reduce stress and allow just a little time for you to spend on yourself.

One of the largest barriers to delegation is when you feel that you are the only one that can do a job right. If that is true, you have just gotten bogged into the detail and it will definitely hamper your ability to be effective on the next skills we will discuss, and that is strategic thinking and planning. You can't be looking forward if your head is always bogged in the details of your job or life.

The other downside is the prevention of others to learn and grow. The reason that anyone becomes good at what they are doing is having the chance to learn that skill, implement that skill and then practice, practice, practice that skill. The pit fall is that once you get so good and comfortable executing one of your great skills, it becomes personally rewarding to show people how good you are at it and thus keep it to yourself. The solution, **give it away**. Let others learn what you have learned. Whether it is giving assignments out in the office or teaching your children how to iron their own clothes or cut the lawn. Just give it away... delegate.

STRATEGIC THINKING AND PLANNING: *OUR NATION*

The higher the entity of power, the more responsibility they have to look into the future to foresee what has to be done today to be prepared for what that future will bring. The average American citizen who is fighting to survive is thinking months or if fortunate enough, can put plans together that might stretch out to several years. Organizations, because of constant changes in products, budgets, markets, technology and so many other critical areas must plan ahead for decades. Our nation's leaders, however, are entrusted to foresee forty, fifty, and even further into the future to ensure we are doing what must be done for us, not only to survive but to prosper.

This could include decisions about climate control, natural resources, energy supply, population changes, educational requirements for future workforce needs, military needs for our future protection, and many other long-range issues that are critical for our survival. Many of these issues are rightfully being debated within our government agencies and legislatures today. This was successfully done in a bipartisan way when in the late sixties, Congress passed the Clean Air Act at a time when industries were polluting the air and our waterways were burning from pollution. Fifty years later, we are benefiting from their strategic thinking. Hopefully, they can think far enough ahead and not get bogged in emotions in addressing the critical issues connected to talent development and the void that may be created by the reduction in white males that must be filled by our changing diverse workforce.

RECOMMENDATIONS

Hopefully, we will have future legislatures in both our nation and states that will put aside their emotional near-term policy issues and start to evaluate our future needs with facts and clear heads. This could mean an honest assessment of our educational institutions to determine if all of our children are being offered the best education that is possible regardless of race, gender, and socioeconomic status. It could be ensuring that later generations have access to proper health care, and financial and career opportunities. This could mean that more manufacturing must be brought back to our country and educational grants offered in areas important for our country's future growth.

One of the most important thoughts for our leaders is to remember that we are not alone on this planet and there are many nations who want to take our leadership role away from us. They must remind themselves that the enemy is not within our boundaries but within our competitive nations.

STRATEGIC THINKING AND PLANNING: *THE ORGANIZATION*

This is an important skill American employees count on their executive team to, not only be strategic in their thinking, but also in their accuracy in predicting the future. The results of their effectiveness could very well define their future employment and career opportunities. Areas of product development, global marketing, technology advancements, marketing strategies, manufacturing decisions, and many other critical areas must be decided with accuracy if the organization is to grow and prosper. Depending on the markets that are involved, could mean thinking decades ahead.

RECOMMENDATIONS

The one area that is justifiably getting more attention is talent development. As our workforce is changing in its diversity, it is incumbent on the executive teams to forecast the talent that will be needed for the future growth of their organization. Decisions then must be made as to the development of this new diverse workforce and examine if they are creating the work environment that will allow this new diverse workforce to thrive, grow, and be productive. These are issues that become much more complicated than future products because it involves people, the most complicated but most important ingredient of any organization's success.

With the knowledge we now have of the diminishing numbers of white males and the increase in the diverse population predicated in our future, many organizations are strategically addressing the leadership void that we will have in the not-so-distant future if this issue is not addressed. Initiatives such as supporting Employee Resource Groups (ERGs), executive mentoring programs, and the forming of Talent Development Departments, all suggest awareness of the future. My only concern is the amount of priority that is being placed on these initiatives.

Since major changes in this area may not be felt for another ten to twenty years, there might be a tendency to address more immediate problems and not put the proper time and resources into the development of their future leadership development efforts. To allow ERGs to form but not giving them the resources to train and grow their members may not be enough to meet the leadership challenges that clearly lie ahead. "The game is about people, everything else is detail" and this issue must soon take a very high priority.

STRATEGIC THINKING AND PLANNING: *THE INDIVIDUAL*

This skill in many organizations is labeled career planning and is often lightly touched upon in possibly an annual career planning session with your boss. In reality, that is probably all your organization should be doing for, after all, it is your career and you are the CEO of your life, responsible for your own career direction and outcome.

RECOMMENDATIONS

Make sure that you schedule at least an annual career planning session with your boss. Even if that session is not a requirement for your manager to have one with you, get on his or her calendar anyway. That session should be merely to get clarification on issues you have and to gain information on career opportunities and requirements. Only you can determine if you want a technical career or an upwardly oriented one. Your boss cannot make those decisions for you nor should you want him or her to do so.

That then falls upon you to make one of the hardest decisions that a person has to make. That is, "What do I want to do with my career and my life?" Very tough decisions, but the sooner you can make them the sooner you can put a development plan together to ensure that you will get to your objectives. Once you decide where you want to take your career, your planning should fall into three stages: short, mid-term, and long-term strategic planning.

SHORT TERM:

An Individual's short-term planning can cover as short of a period as a few months to no longer than a year in the future. These plans should be ones that cover how to become more efficient in your current job, including any skills training needed, and what image changes you should be addressing (remember the area of the image has three times the weight of performance in your competitiveness in being promoted).

RECOMMENDATIONS

In accessing your image, it is important to evaluate if you are creating the image that the job you are seeking requires. This is when you must consider what changes you must make to meet those future requirements. Of course, it could be in the area of dress but also could be in the development of the new skills the next job will require. An example would be if you are now an individual contributor and the next position you are seeking is a management position. You must ask yourself if you are showing your ability and willingness to help, motivate and take a leadership role with your fellow individual contributor. These are the skills a future sponsor will be looking for, not just how well you are doing your current assignment and how professional your dress code is.

In the area of exposure, your strategies might be to put on your calendar what upper-level managers and executives you should plan to meet with to discuss your career. This could be via lunch or even a zoom meeting if needed. Planning in this area could include, deciding what special projects for which you might be willing to volunteer, what retirement or promotion parties you need to attend, and maybe even what professional or community organization you need to join.

MID-TERM:

Planning in this area should be beyond six months to one to two years. During this period, you might decide what new social activities you might want to learn or in which you would like to get involved. It could be to take golfing lessons or to join a tennis team. Maybe it is to find out more about the symphony or plan to attend a musical or a ballet. Other activities such as learning bridge, going skiing, sailing, and whatever activities you think you might like to try should start to appear on your "to do" list.

RECOMMENDATIONS

In your decision to decide what new activities you might want to take on, a few things you might want to keep in mind. First and foremost, choose those new activities that you will have some enjoyment in learning. There is no reason in your effort to take on self-growth that you can't enjoy the process. Also, while choosing a new activity, it might be a good thing to check with your significant other if they would like to join you. Remember, at the top of the social pyramid many activities are couple oriented. Golf, tennis, bridge, and dinner parties are just a few activities that fit into this category. The higher you choose to ascend on the socio-economic pyramid, the busier you most likely will become. Many activities might be a good source for your relationship and a chance to spend some fun time with your partner.

The same logic applies in picking community activities for which you might want to become involved. All community volunteer activities will automatically expand your network but if you have some interest in that activity, it will keep your interest or even create a passion. This might be, for example, volunteering for the PTA because you have children going to that school or volunteering with the National Heart Association because you have a member of your family that has a condition in this area. Being a representative for your organization in your community, expanding your personal network, enhancing your personal growth, and making a legitimate contribution by giving back can be a win/win/win/win situation.

LONG TERM:

This is a plan that can take you out as far as five years or more. It might be planning to go back to school to get more education via night school, weekends, or the Internet. It might involve ensuring that you have sound financial plans in place for your family's future.

Remember, strategic planning is the ability to look out into the future, decide where you want to be, and then determine what you have to do to be prepared to compete with others who will also want that position in five years. What you don't want to happen is to start that development process one year before that job might be in the offering and then have to make up for things in one year that you could have started or completed years before. Effective strategic planning is the process that will reduce that from happening. This is an area where you want to put away those statements of "One day I'm going to learn……," or I've always wanted to learn how to……," or I've always said that one day I was going to….."

Strategic thinking is a skill that just might force you into not just talking about it. Remember, the game is about not just having a good plan, it is about execution: As the saying goes, "Just do it!"

CHAPTER TWENTY-ONE

THE DREAM I HAVE FOR AMERICA

CHASING YOUR "AMERICAN DREAM"

We have always heard about the American dream and understand that it is not only an often-quoted phase but is something that we, as Americans, all wish for ourselves and our loved ones. But before it can be reached, it is important to not only understand what it is but more importantly, know what it takes to get there.

Your American Dream can be and is whatever you want it to be. It may be to take a leadership role on your specific "reservation" or to live in mainstream America and make an impact on the lives of individuals that resided in all of our many beautiful racial, ethnic, religious, and sexual-oriented communities. Maybe we can define a true American as a person that loves and appreciates the contributions that emanate from all of our various communities. After all, this is the core of America's greatness. These racial and ethnic communities have been and will always be the nuclear source of our collective strength. We will always have and will continually need the outpouring of the creative richness that comes out of all of our cultural communities.

We have asked the world to send us their "tired, poor and huddled masses yearning to breathe free." The assumption made by us and the world was, we would provide a place for their safe landing, usually in a community of people just like themselves. However, when that person becomes comfortable and when and if they choose to do so, we will then accept them and their talents into the mainstream where even bigger "dreams" might come true. In essence, we will eventually bring them into the melting pot, which is the blending of all of America's cultures. This, of course, adds to the richness of any one culture and will make that person not just an Irish, Italian or Black American but a total or as the label suggests, an All-American. This will give that person the knowledge and savvy of the combined best of all of us. We have committed to taking people from every part of the world and turning that person into the smartest, best educated, most moral, ethical, truthful, respectful, and committed defenders of freedom and human rights that we possibly can.

Is it any wonder why we Americans think we are the best in the world? Within our borders, we have representation of the entire world and are finally beginning to tap into the contributions that all Americans have the potential of making. The question is, can we continually do it at the casual pace that we have been addressing this issue if we are to keep ahead of our domestic and global competitors?

There are strong indicators that we are falling behind in that regard. Many might say that America has become less focus on the future because we are far too busy with our internal squabbles. It's like our egos have allowed us to forget about the rising competitiveness of the rest of the world. We are thinking about bringing the old America back instead of strategically thinking about what the world will be like fifty years from now and how we should be preparing a new America for that future world.

Instead of looking back, we should be looking ahead. If we want to keep everyone's financial portfolios strong, we better be thinking about making our children strong and knowledgeable. Maybe then we might be able to compete with China, Russia, Europe, and India in what they and many other emerging nations are doing with their children's development. We cannot lose sight that our successful future lays in a nation of diverse people and just not the white male population.

In 1963, I was fortunate to be there when Dr. Martin Luther King made history when he told us about his dream. In the six decades since that speech, many of his dreams, if not having totally come true, have at least been advanced to some degree. Maybe it's time to recharge his dream of America and advance that dream forward for another six decades. With your permission, I would like to take a crack at the dream I have for our future America. Before I do, however, it's important to review what might be some of America's future challenges.

THE RESPONSIBILITY OF BEING THE MAJOR DEFENDER OF DEMOCRACY

My view of future America is one that we collectively understand our responsibility to uphold democracy and its principles. We must ensure future immigrants and those that are currently on their journey to mainstream America, that they have the right to choose their individual life objectives and to be free in making the choices they feel will allow them to reach those objectives. This is the America we have and this is the America we must preserve. We just have to get better at making all of this happen faster.

As a nation, we have made the commitment to not only run our country as a democracy but to also defend that political philosophy around the world. We are aware that every nation, under sovereignty, has the right to choose its own form of government. Many nations are asking themselves, "Should we have a strong autocratic leader to take us through times of peril or should we allow the will of the people to decide their fate?" We, of course, will always champion democracy and try our best to lead those indecisive nations to what we feel is the correct path. We have fought in many wars and many of our ancestors have died defending our right to remain free and live under a democratic form of government. With events of early 2021, such as citizens not accepting voting results and the storming of the U.S. Capitol, these events might have given the doubters of democracy more ammunition. Although England was the first to give the world the concept of people rule, we have been the most aggressive to show that it works and in trying to get the world to adopt it. We might have faltered a little but I am confident that we will not fail in this important mission.

The current war between Russia, an autocracy, and Ukraine, a democracy, is pitying the two forms of governments more openly than since World War II. It has united the free world to take a stand against authoritarian aggression with the support given to Ukraine by the U.S. and other NATO nations. As of this writing, we are watching to see how much support other authoritarian nations such as China and authoritarian leaning nations such as India and Saudi Arabia will come to Russia's aid. But there is little doubt that war between the two forms of government is on the table and is costing the lives of many people in making the determination as to which will prevail.

WHY SHOULD WE DEFEND DEMOCRACY AROUND THE WORLD?

Our logic is sound with this issue. If the world order operates by the same set of democratic and human rights policies and more, we know we have an advantage. We have proven to be one of the better players in that environment than most. Why? Because we have the representation of the world within our borders and are beginning to understand that we must get the best from everyone that is sent to us if we are to remain a strong nation. By tapping into every American's creativity, courage, morality, strength, ambition, perspectives, values, and general wisdom and richness of life experiences; there will be nothing that is impossible for us, as a nation, to do.

The advantage of being the leader of the free world (when and if the entire world eventually becomes free), will be not having to attack the challenges facing the world's humanitarian issues alone. We will be able to do it in partnership with that new, future, democratic world. With the Covid-19 pandemic, we can see the benefit that would be gained by the entire world if every country could communicate from the same political foundation and have solid bonds of cooperation with each other.

Much work, however, lies ahead for us if we still want to stay in the leadership role of championing freedom and human rights. Let's hope those basic principles by which we were founded will not fade or die but instead, keep us on the path of fulfilling that commitment. As a nation, we can only be as strong as our weakest link and the pandemic has laid bare many of our weak links. So, let's first level the playing field for all Americans in the areas of equal justice, education, financial support, and job/business opportunities.

The next important step is to share the rules of our system with everyone and then, "Let the games begin." If we can do these things, I see a nation that will no longer overlook the potential of any child or an organization failing to develop its total future diverse leadership pool. I see a nation that finally fulfills Dr. King's dream of us not judging people by race, gender, religion, or sexual orientation but will judge the content of everyone's character. I see a nation that allows every person to be able to maximize their potential and when and if we can do this, I see a nation that will be able to compete with any country in the world.

From the days I had crosses burned on the lawns of my homes, I have seen amazing change and progress in America. I don't think that progress is going to stop. As a matter of fact, I'm sure of it. You see, I not only have a dream, but I also have the feeling that America will one day be the America of which we all have dreamed and pledged. One, not only of "liberty and justice for all" but equal opportunity for all as well. This can only be done by teaching the "rules of the game" to everyone.

THE WISH I HAVE FOR EVERY AMERICAN

Thank heavens for living in a nation that allows individuals to choose their own destinies. If their choice is that they prefer to play out their lives in their designated community, then that is a choice where a person can improve their community by bringing their personal leadership skills and life knowledge to truly make a difference. This can, of course, be rewarding by making an impact and building upon the gains and contributions so many others have done on the journey toward equality for all. It also allows this contribution to be made in the comfortable surroundings of family, friends, and history. There can't be anything wrong with that choice. The opportunity to provide for your family and at the same time be able to stay in a world that is familiar to you and be around people that you love should provide the happiness that all of us seek. If this is your choice, you've made a great choice and of course, good luck on your journey.

For those who might decide they want to try playing in the mainstream, the choice to do so will open up additional options in your life. By playing by mainstream rules and if your career objectives include upward mobility, self-change will be a constant factor in your life. That change will continue until you decide that you have advanced high enough. When you decide that you and your family no longer want to change, then your upward movement will more than likely stop; but when it does, you will hopefully be in a place where you can live out the remainder of your life in comfort and happiness. The key is, you are in total control as to when that will happen. You call all of those shots.

An important thing to remember is the choice to remain on an upward career path puts you in competition with all other dedicated game players. To win in this arena, it is critical to learn the rules and execute via those rules better than everyone else. As your career advances upwardly, the rule requirements will continue to change at the various higher levels so you must always be ready to adjust, learn and grow. It is also important to understand that the higher you set your goals, the more dedicated, motivated, and skillful your competitors will be. You won't win every one of your battles, but if you stay dedicated, motivated, and continue learning new skills; with patience, your time will come. Never stop learning, never stop trying if upward mobility is what you want.

AM I THERE YET?

Maybe a final question to be discussed is how do you know when you get to Mainstream America? As an African-American, I have been asked many times in my life why I refer to myself as a Black or African-American. They follow with the comment that they are Irish or Italian, but they think of themselves just as American, and then ask "Why can't you and your people do the same?" Of course, one answer is, many of us feel that we are not treated as equal Americans or feel that we are not as respected as other citizens. Thus, we put the African to our title, ensuring that we are recognized as being a part of our nation. When any group of our citizens feel separated and don't trust that mainstream America will welcome them into its world by giving them an equal chance to succeed, then they simply stay where they know they are welcome.

This may be a good way to gauge our nation's or anyone's personal progress on the journey to America's mainstream. When I, as a Black American, can change that label in my own mind and the minds of my white fellow citizens, from being seen as a Black American to just being an American who just happens to be Black, it could be a measuring gauge as to where anyone might be on their journey to the American mainstream. Many other very proud ethnic groups have ditched their ethnic identification label (Italian-American, Irish-America, etc.) And most, outside of their reservation communities, are seen as just being American. It is slowly starting to happen with mixed-race children. With the "browning" of America, and with several generations in the future, more of our children will see themselves as American (Who proudly happens to be (fill in the blank). The speed of this happening will depend on both the acceptance of the mainstream towards African-Americans as well as the number of African-Americans who might be willing to take that journey. The same of course applies to the Hispanic, Asian, and all other cultural communities as well.

What this says about our country is skin color is still a factor in many Americans' evaluation of people. Does this mean that dark-skinned Americans cannot be successful? Of course not. Character, talent, and contributions will always be the final measure by which every American will be judged. It just says that skin color is one of those things in our country that many of our fellow citizens still have a hard time with. This puts "skin color" on the list, along with gender, disabilities, and sexual orientation, that must be overcome in today's America. However, everything on that list can be overcome with character, talent, and contributions.

On Dr. Martin L. King's birthday, I was thinking of how could anyone make such a giant contribution to our nation again. We know that George Washington started our nation on its journey, that Abraham Lincoln saved it for all of us and Dr. King set us on the path that will allow us to survive and prosper in the future if we will only listen and practice what he had to say. His "I have a dream" message has had such a powerful effect on our nation and such a meaningful personal effect on my life, I shall leave his words etched in immortality. I can, however, pass on his message in the form of a wish. Here is my wish list.

I WISH:

- *That all people of color who want to exercise their freedom to join mainstream America gain the knowledge and courage to make the choices needed to reach their life goals;*
- *That every woman who wishes to gain equal status in the nation they have helped make the greatest in the world, continue to move forward with fortitude and persistence to eventually level the playing field for both genders;*
- *That every person with a different sexual orientation will continue their fight for all the freedoms enjoyed by all Americans and be able to live a life of truth to themselves and not have to come out of closets which we, as a society, have forced them into;*
- *That the members of all racial and ethnic communities gain the compassion to understand why any member of their group might want to live and contribute to mainstream America; and that all of us will give them our blessings for a successful journey;*
- *That white America, both those who have mainstreamed and those who have chosen to stay on the white male reservation, gain the foresight and openness to accept a changing America and open their hearts and minds to accept America as it has become today, and positively embrace the future changes that are inevitable for our nation.*

I don't know if this is the time in our nation's history when we start to realize that the world is getting smaller and much more competitive; and that we begin to also realize that "the enemy is out there, not among us."

We can after the events of January 6, 2020, still see that we have a long way to go. But in honor of Dr. King, I will keep his hope alive. I Dream that we, as Americans, can each take personal responsibility to truly make us a "United" America. I know if we try, we can make it happen.

The journey to mainstream America is a difficult and challenging one for anyone to consider but for anyone who chooses to take it on, I can personally attest that it can be exciting and fun. If this is your choice, buckle up your seat belts and get ready for a bumpy but very enjoyable, exciting, and rewarding ride. I would personally recommend giving it a try, but like everything in your life, it's your choice. Godspeed on your journey!

Harvey J. Coleman
President
Coleman Management Consultants, Inc.
5226 Forest Springs Drive
Dunwoody, Ga. 30338
Phone: (404) 234-0683
e-mail: cmc@hcoleman.com
website: www.hcoleman.com